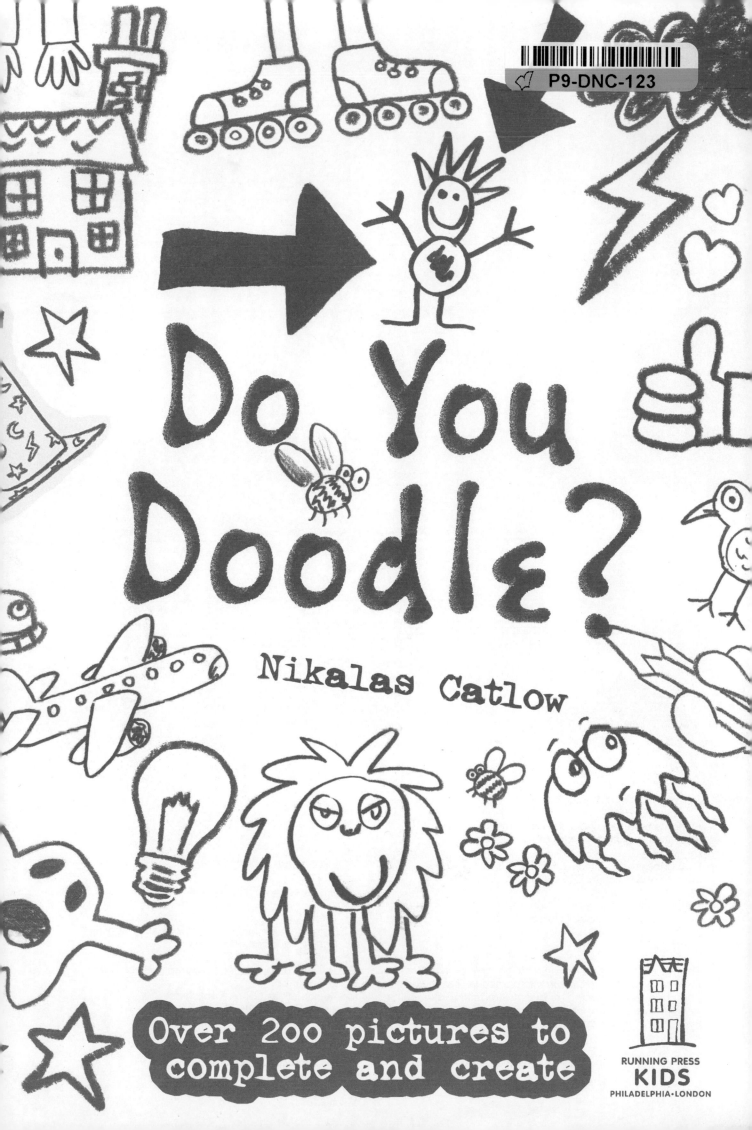

Do You Doodle?

Nikalas Catlow

Over 200 pictures to complete and create

RUNNING PRESS
KIDS
PHILADELPHIA·LONDON

First published in Great Britain by Buster Books,
an imprint of Michael O'Mara Books Limited, 2005

First published in the United States
by Running Press Book Publishers, 2007

Printed in China

21   20   19
Digit on the right indicates the number of this printing

ISBN: 978-0-7624-2927-1

Illustrated by Nikalas Catlow for Amy P.

This book may be ordered by mail from the publisher.
Please include $2.50 for postage and handling.
But try your bookstore first!

This edition published by Running Press Kids,
an imprint of
Running Press Book Publishers
2300 Chestnut Street,
Philadelphia, PA 19103-4371

Visit us on the web!
www.runningpress.com

Draw any idea in your head.

How do you feel?

Build a house.

Look out!

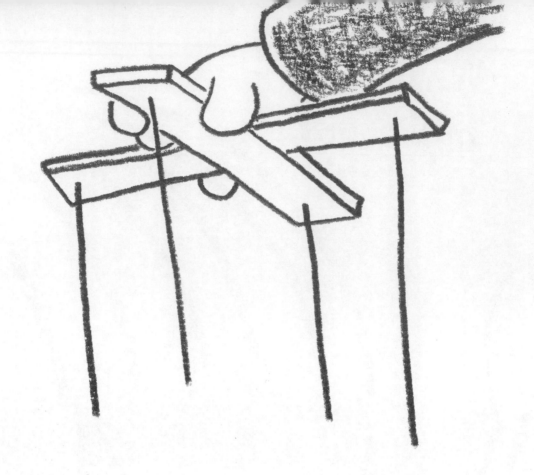

Make a puppet.

Make the genie appear.

Everyone smile!

Ants in your pants!

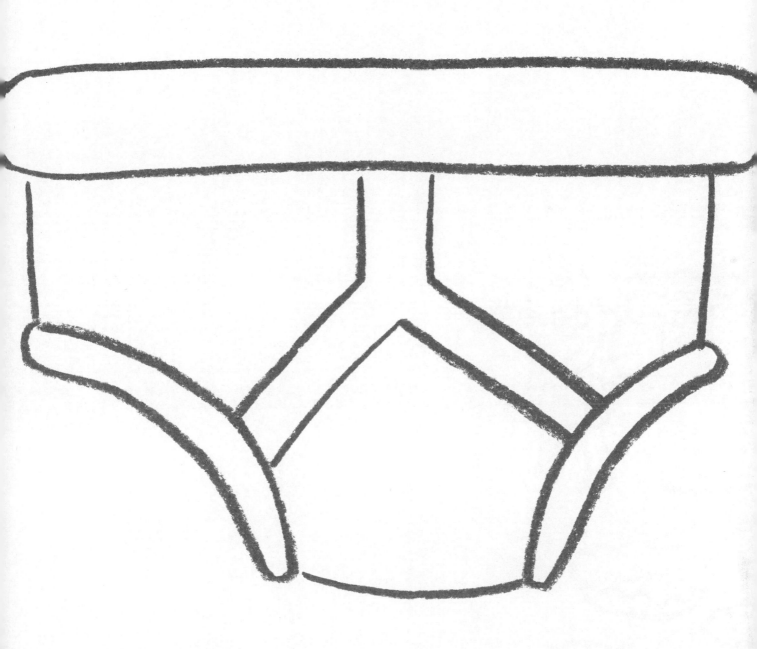

Throw the custard pies.

Make a pile of junk.

Which are slugs and which are snails?

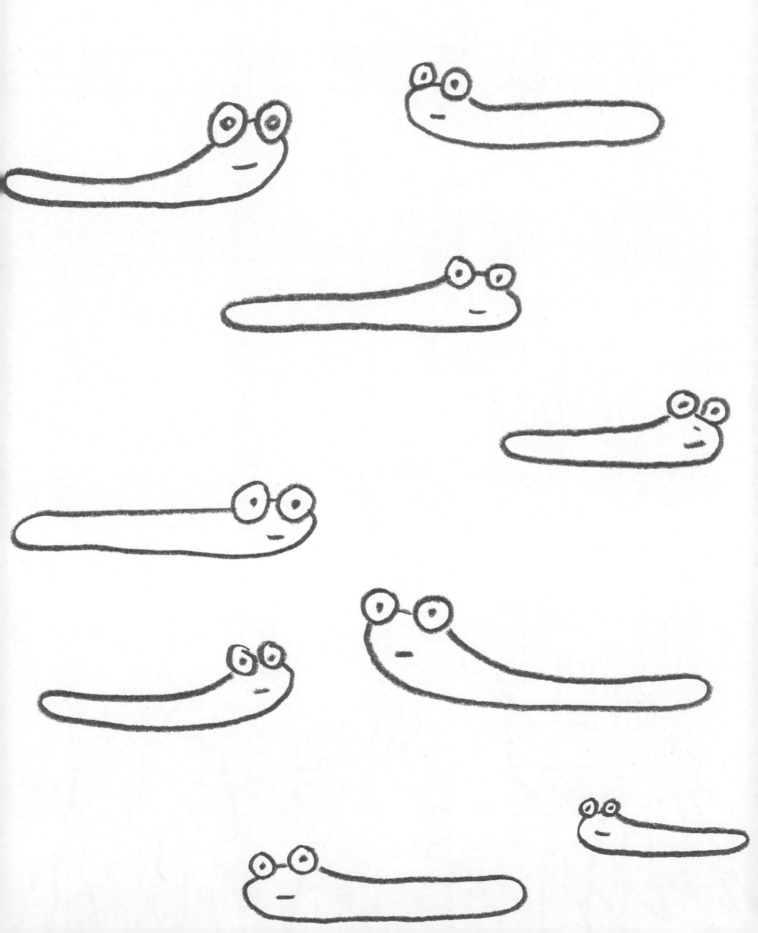

Fantastic fireworks!

Open the parachutes!

Three... Two... One...
Liftoff!

We're surrounded!

Help me escape.

Wrap me in bandages.

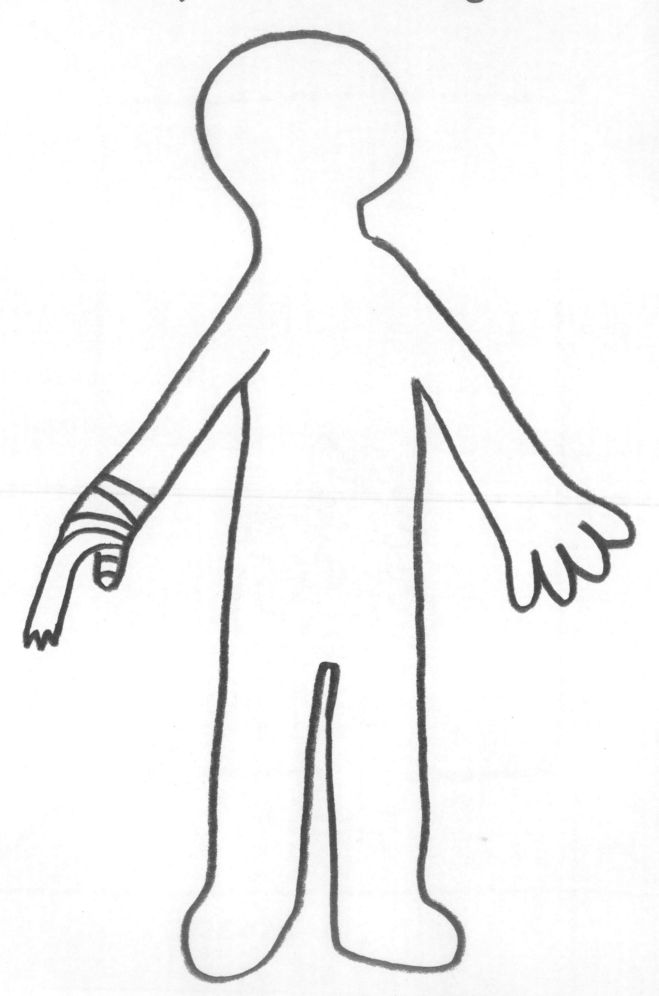

What can you feel?

Have a picnic.

Who's looking at whom?

Help me get down.

Put some candles
on the cake.

What kind of eggs are in the nest?

What's that smell?

What's that noise?

Put on a show.

How much can you carry?

Make a swarm.

Pull me along.

Lift me up.

Charm the snakes from the baskets.

What's in the web?

Who's behind the bushes?

Beware of the sea monster!

A can of worms.

Everything's topsy turvy.

Make a loud BANG!

Hang up hats
and coats.

Decorate the room
for a party.

Fill the pot to
make a spell.

What's in
your stocking?

Put some photos in your album.

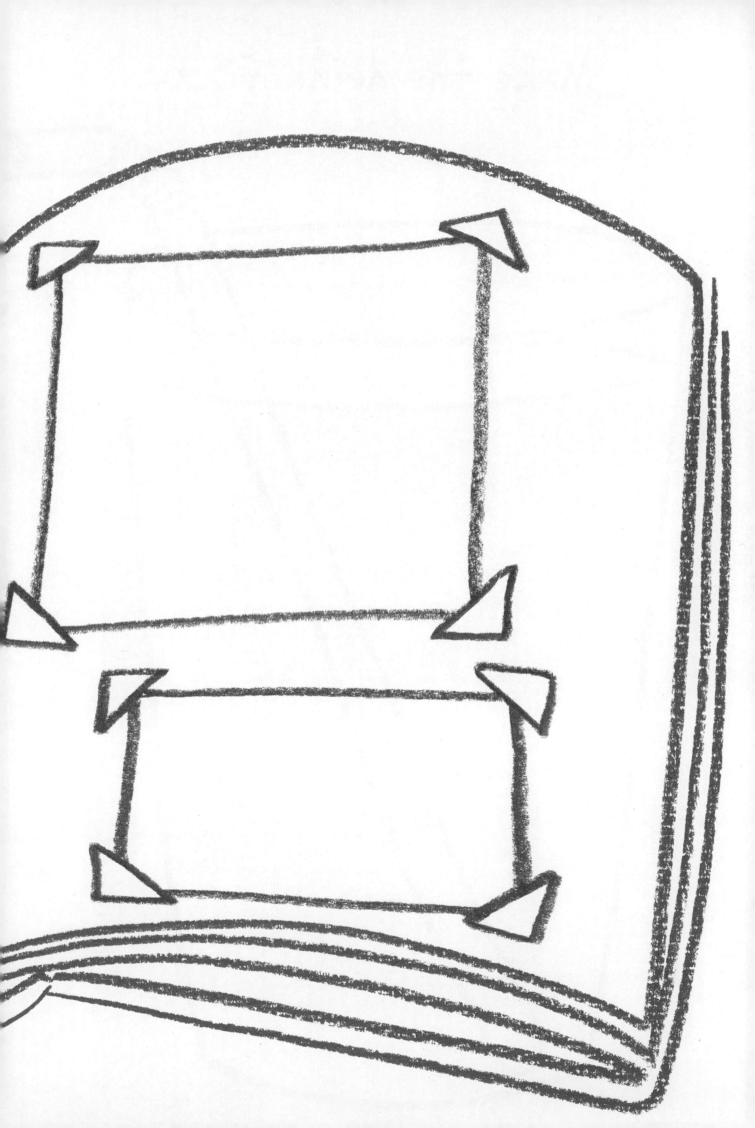

Make the drink fizzy.

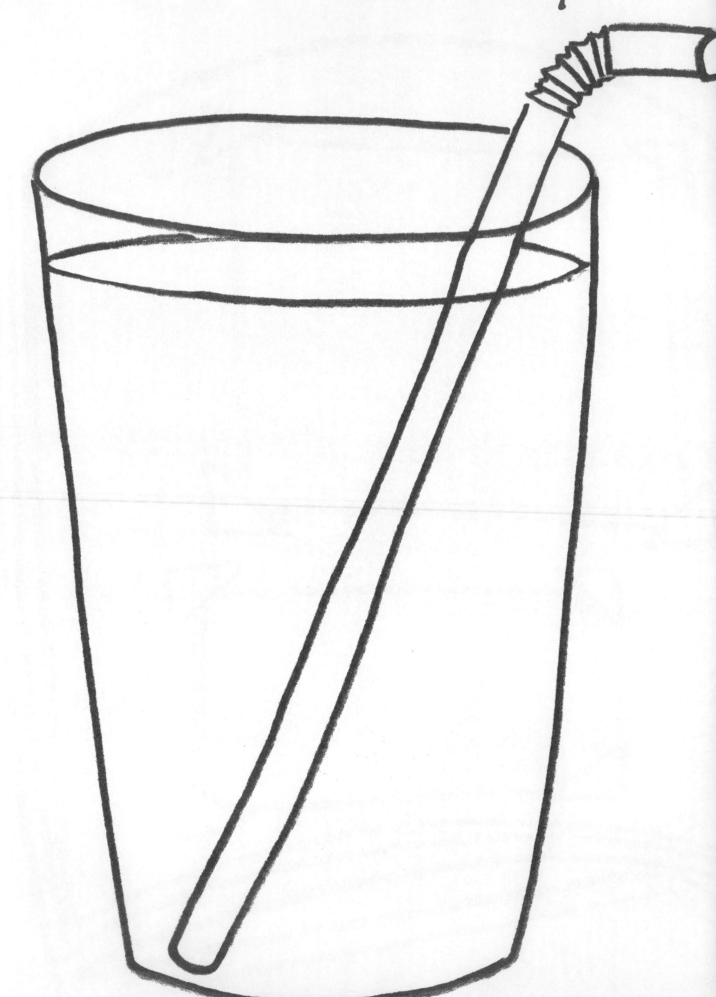

Create a crazy hairstyle.

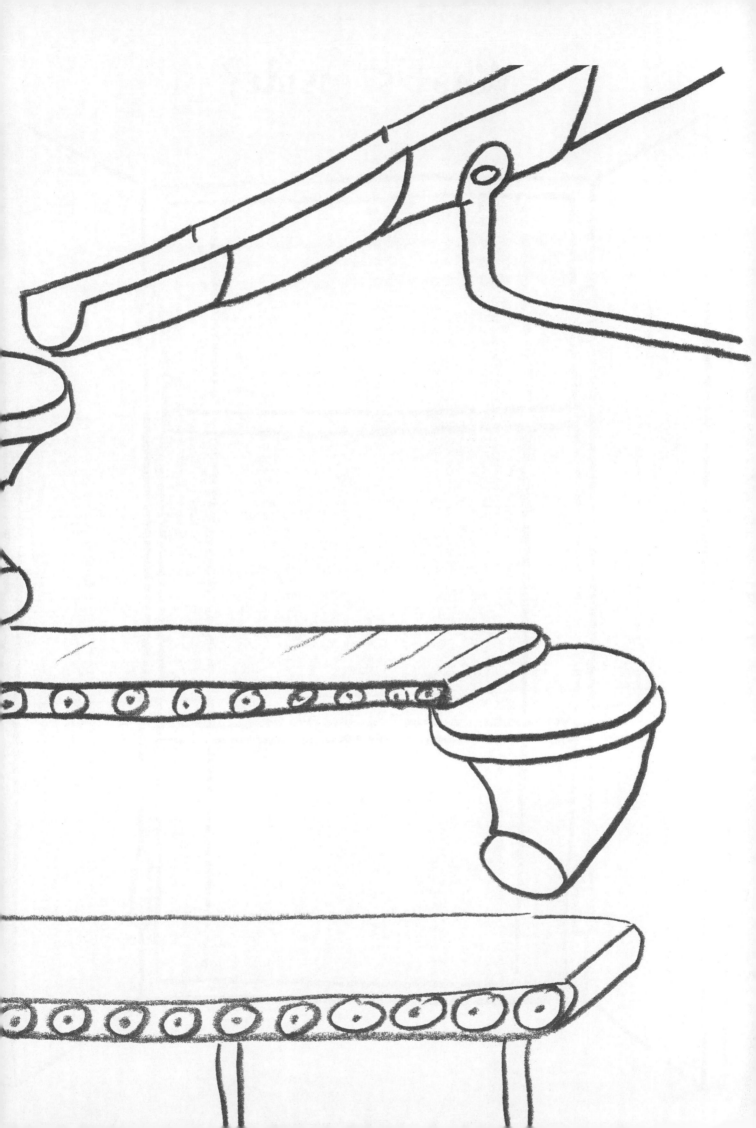

What's inside?

Make a tasty dessert.

Put the vehicles on.

What's on television?

Wrap the presents.

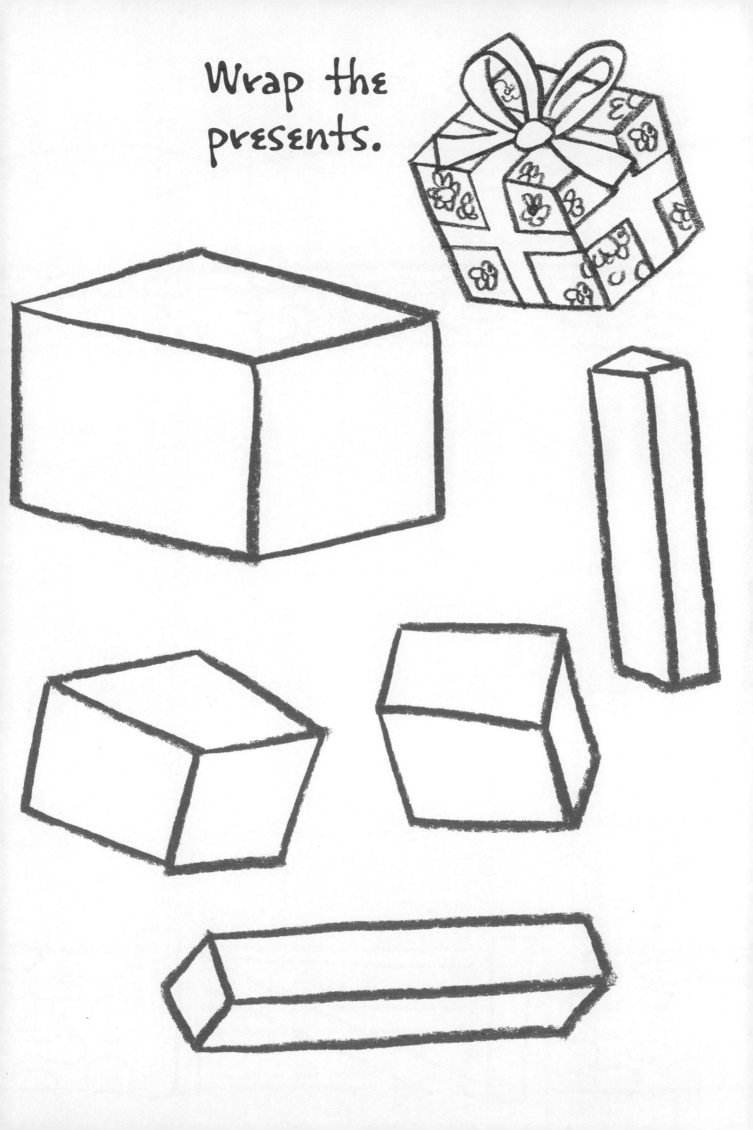

Who's in the field?

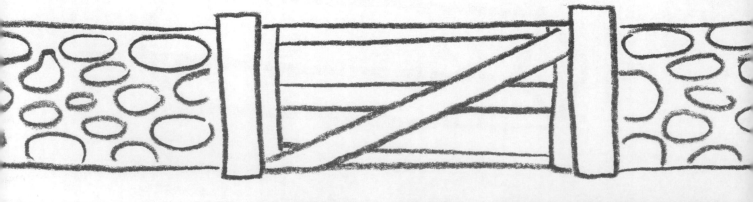

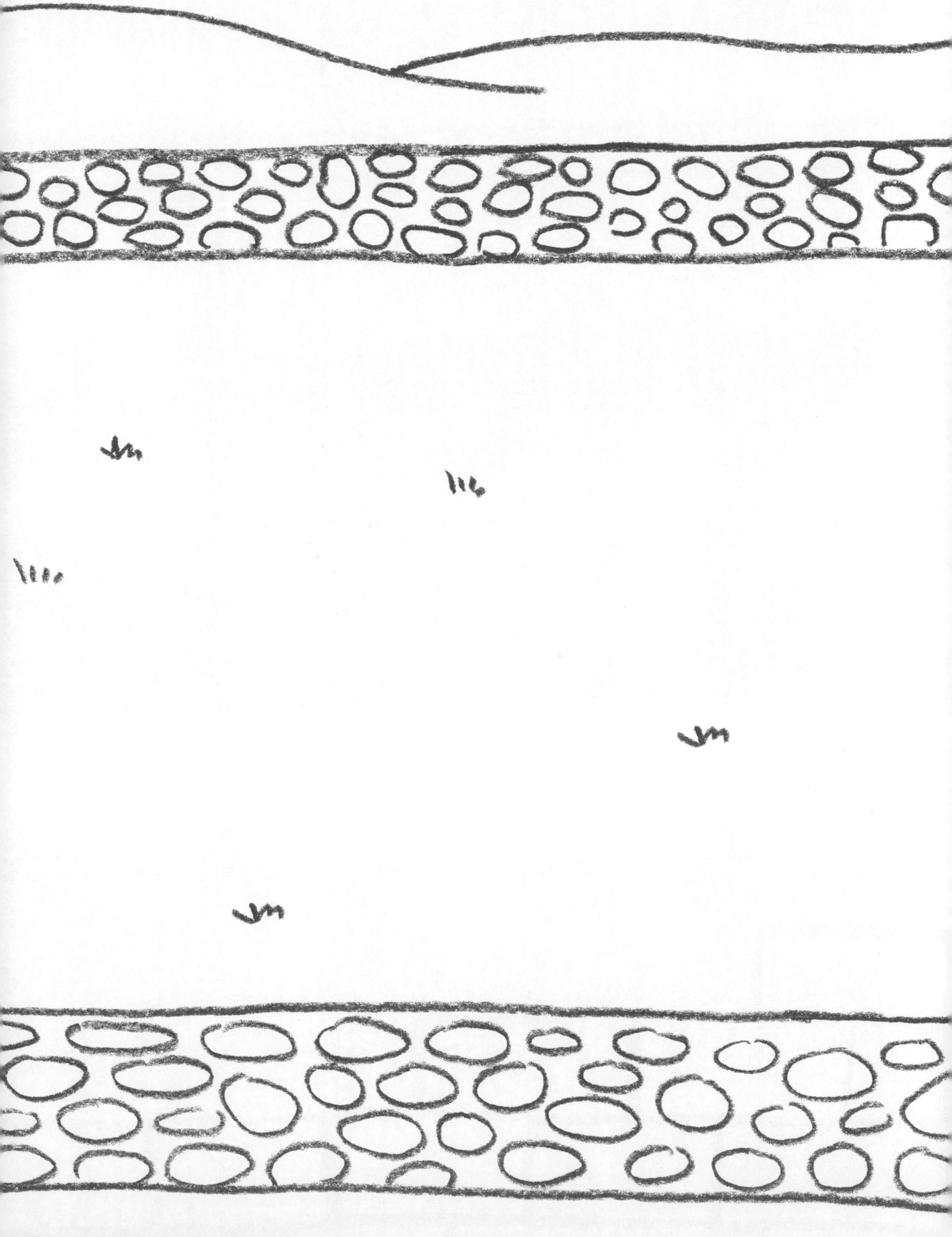

Build a wall.

Decorate the egg.

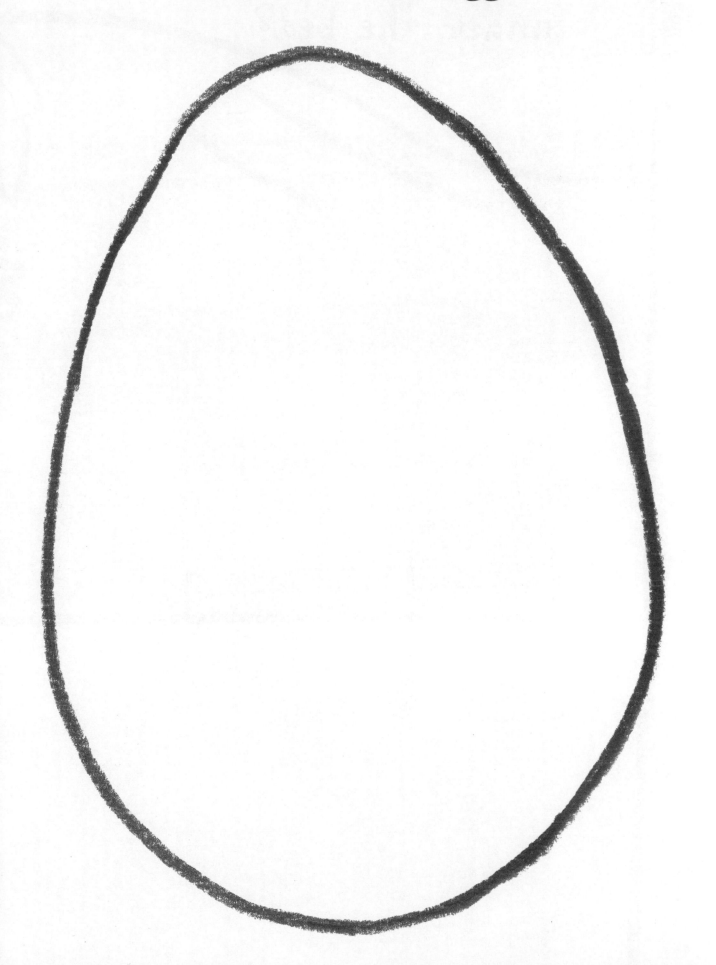

Is there a monster
under the bed?

Whose noses?

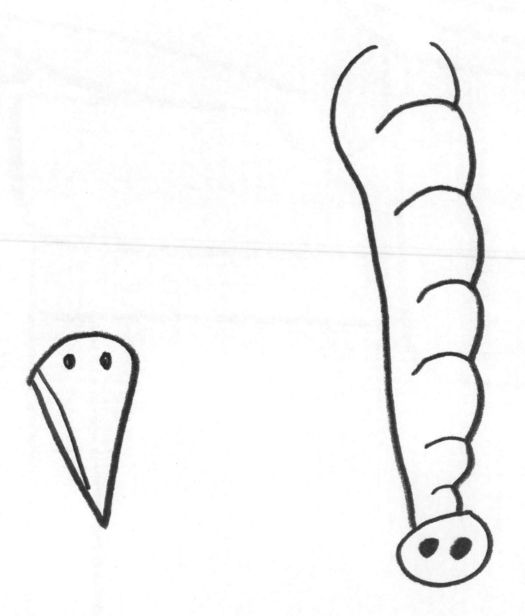

Put some holes in the cheese.

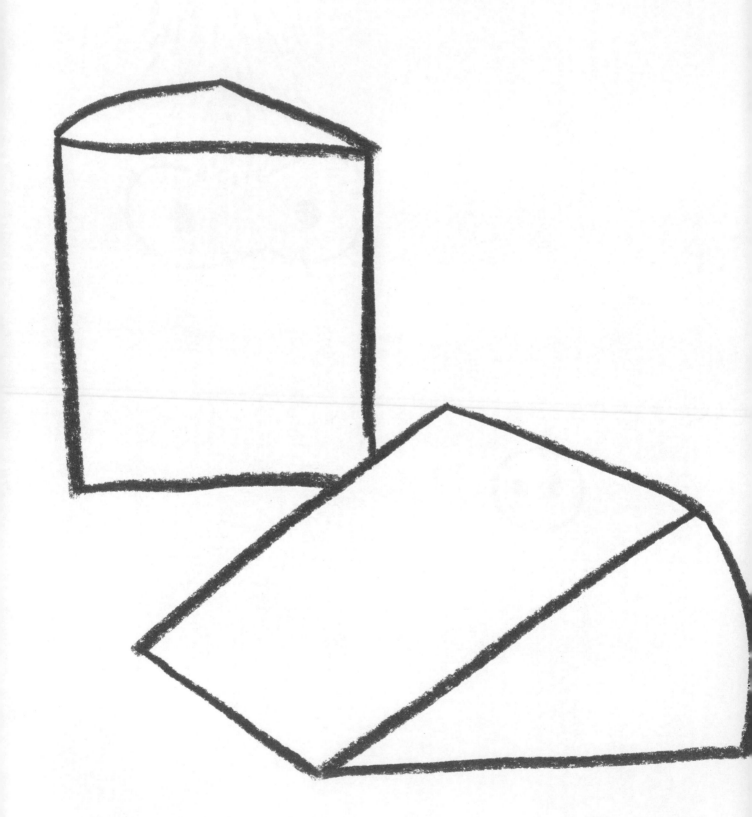

What's in the secret hiding place?

I can see it!

I can see it!

What can you jump over?

Design a T-shirt.

What's in the wash?

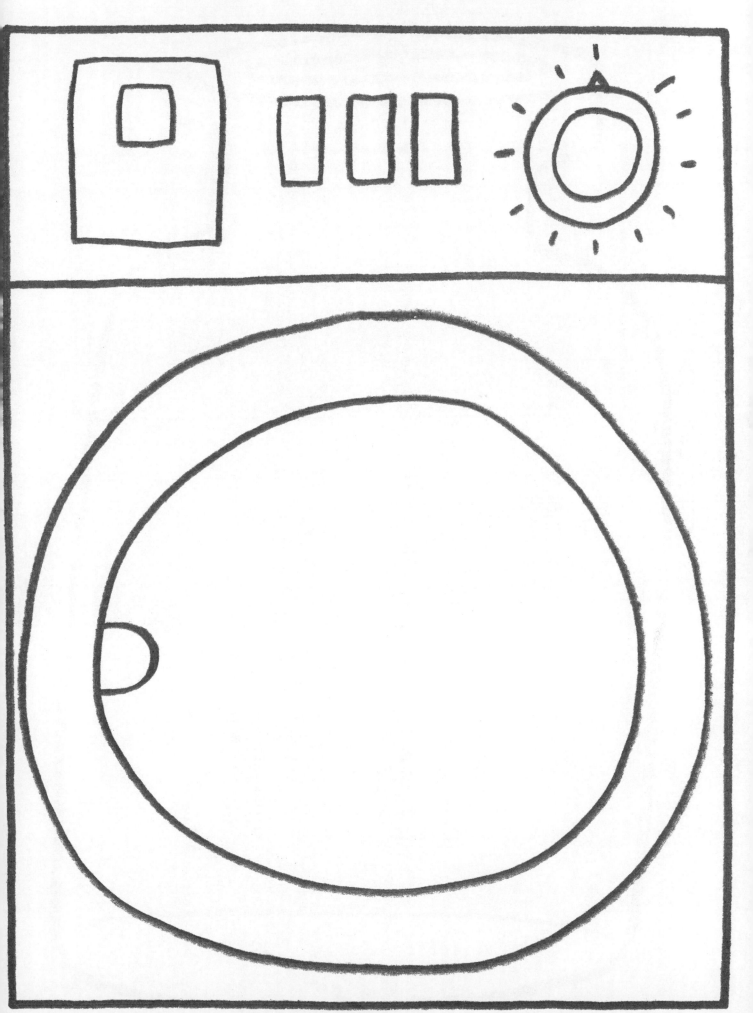

Fill the jar with cookies.

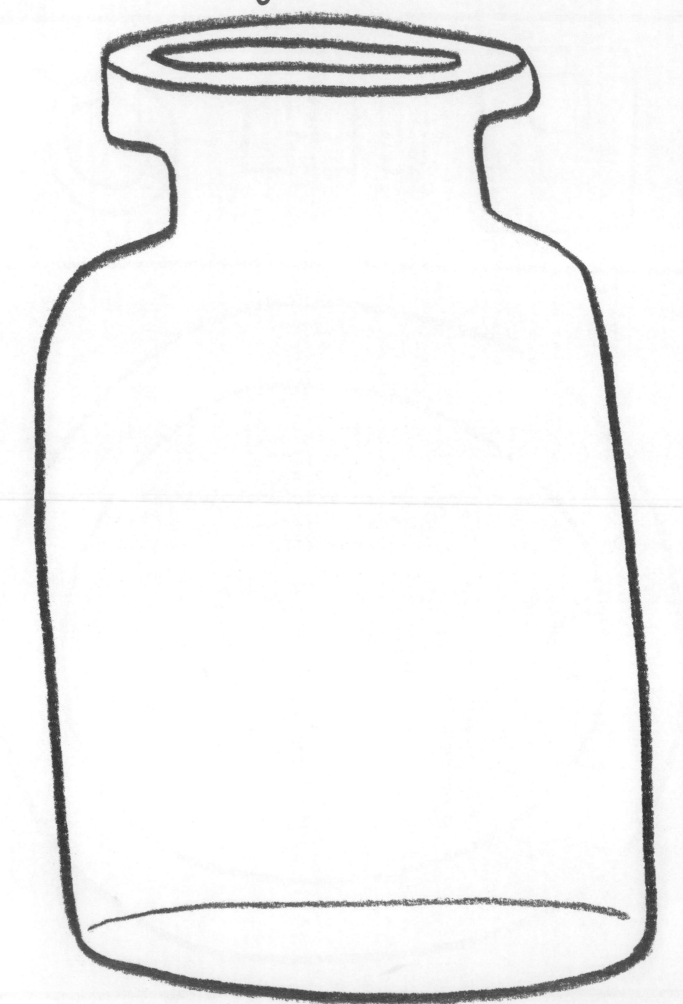

Magnify the ants.

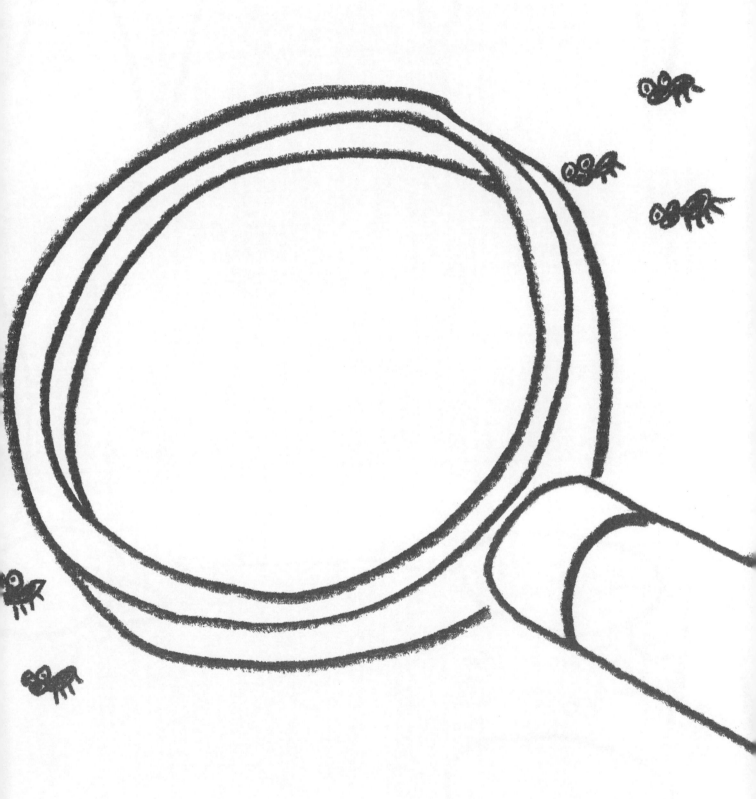

What's in my pouch?

What is the
bird-watcher watching?

What do you see in the crystal ball?

Fill the box with
anything you want.

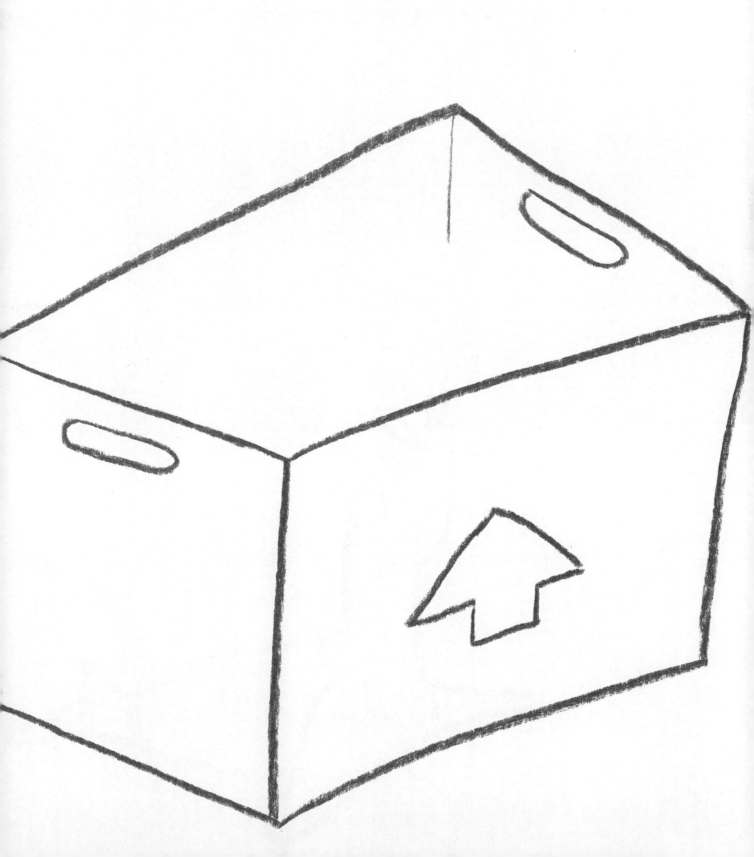

Balance something on
the seal's nose.

Put legs and wings on the insects.

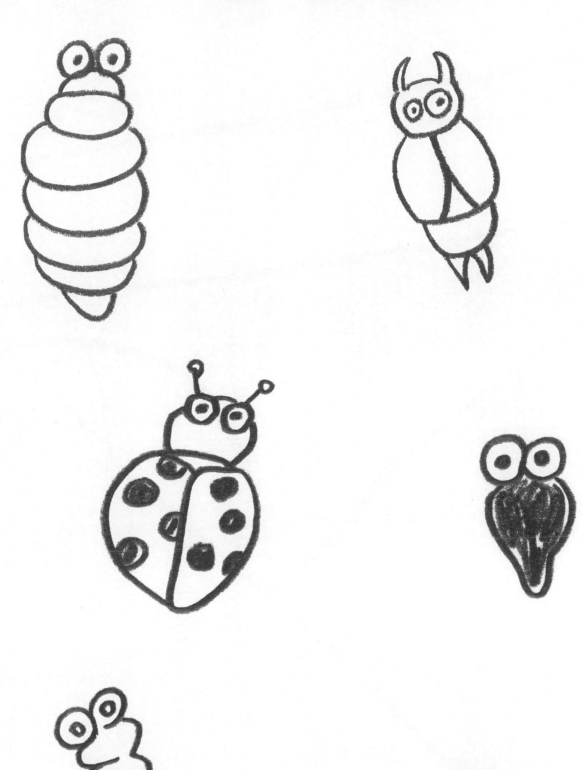

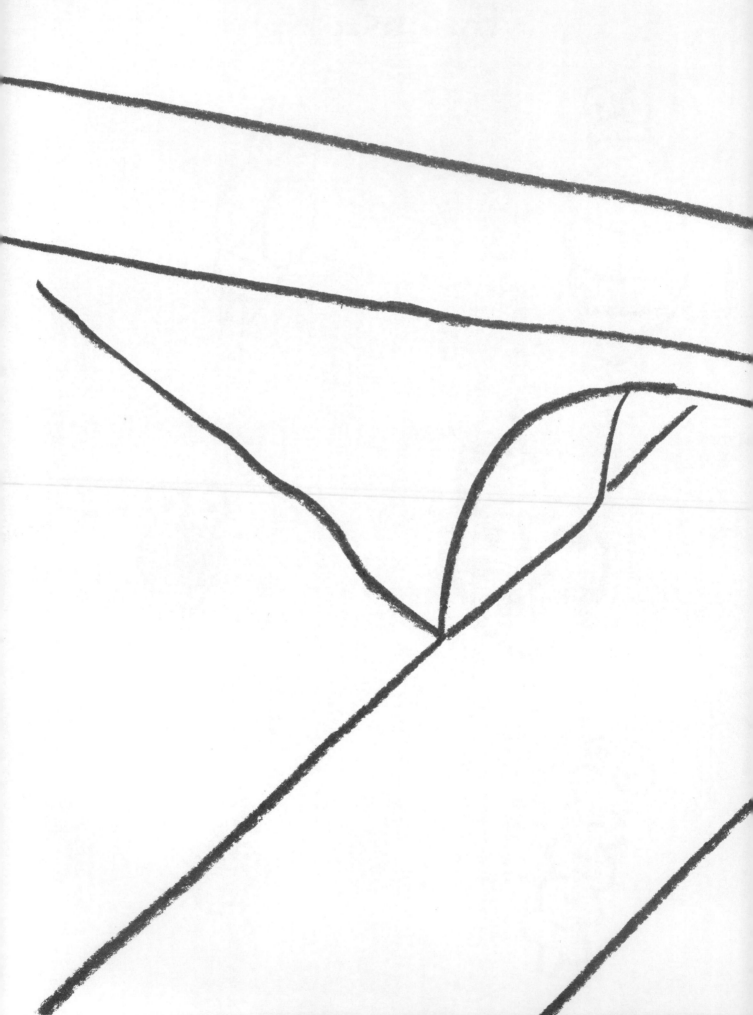

What goes under?

What do you take to bed?

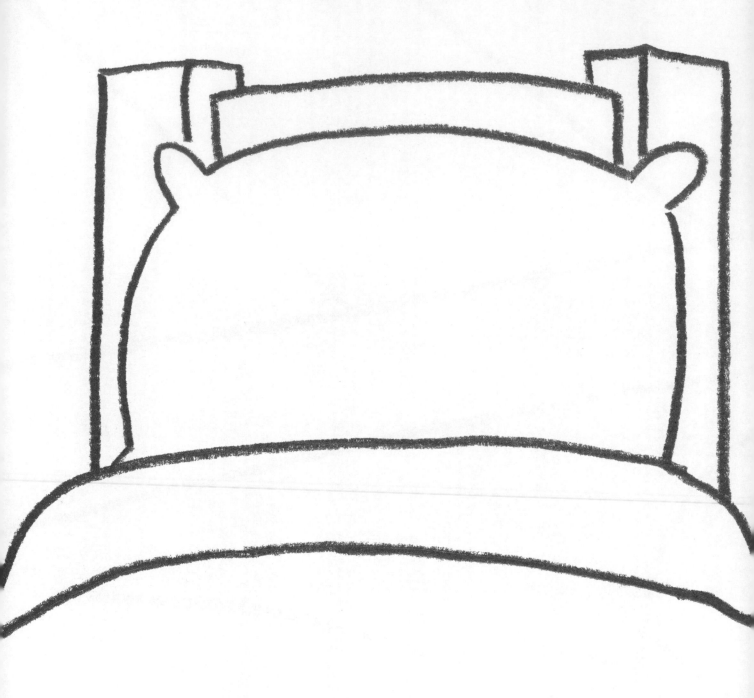

Give me
a tattoo.

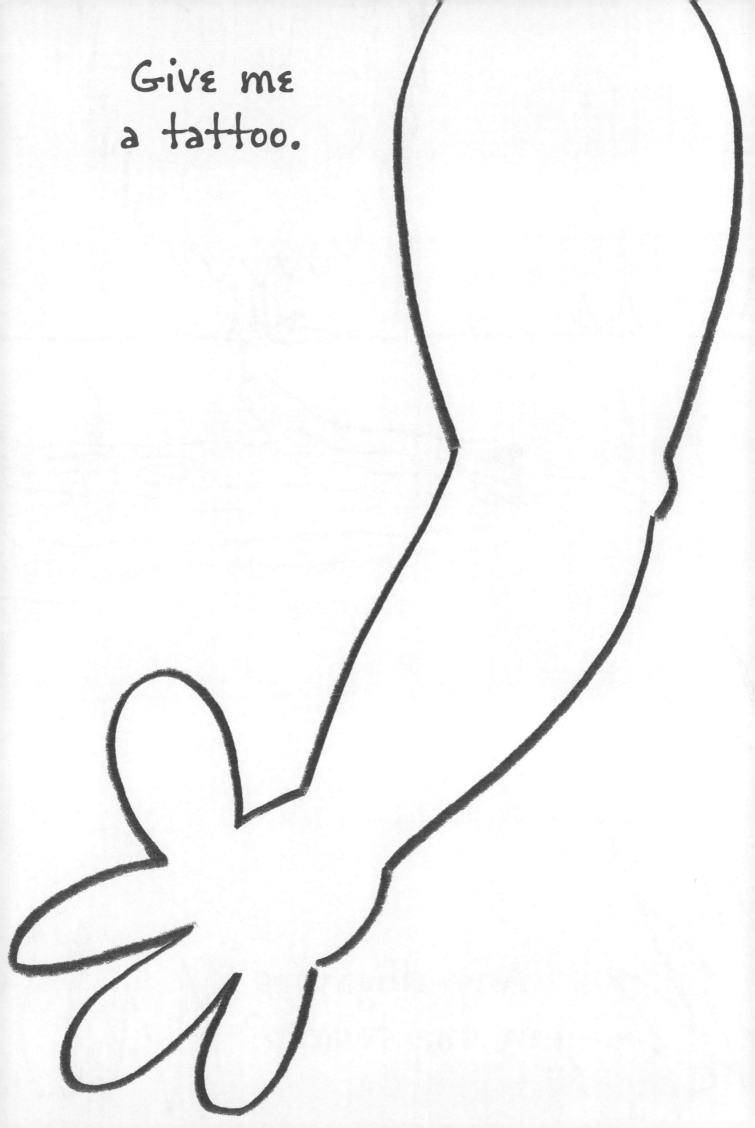

Any alligators
in the swamp?

The zebra and the
tiger need stripes.

Give the pig a mud bath.

What's in the attic?

What are you scared of?

Finish the pattern.

Whose houses?

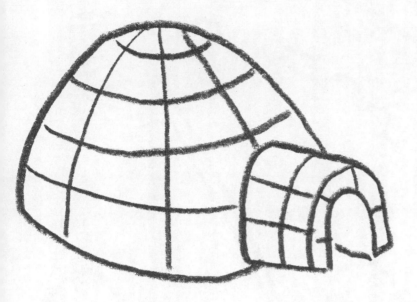

What did they catch?

What do caterpillars turn into?

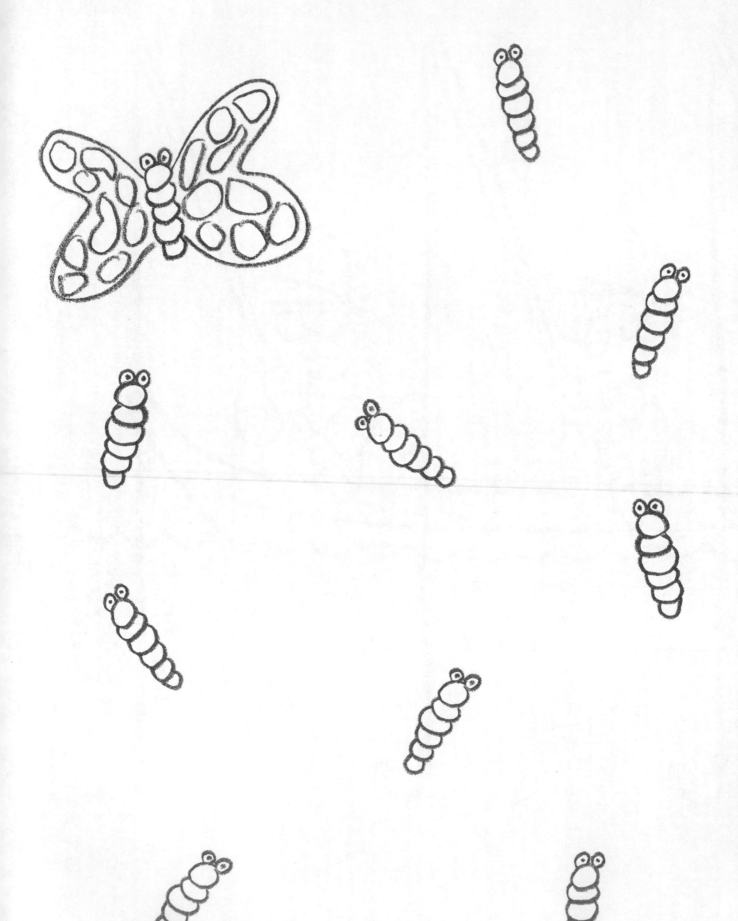

Put the fire out!

I'll huff and I'll puff...

What am I lifting?

Show my skeleton.

X-RAY

machine

Fly the kite.

What is the cat chasing?

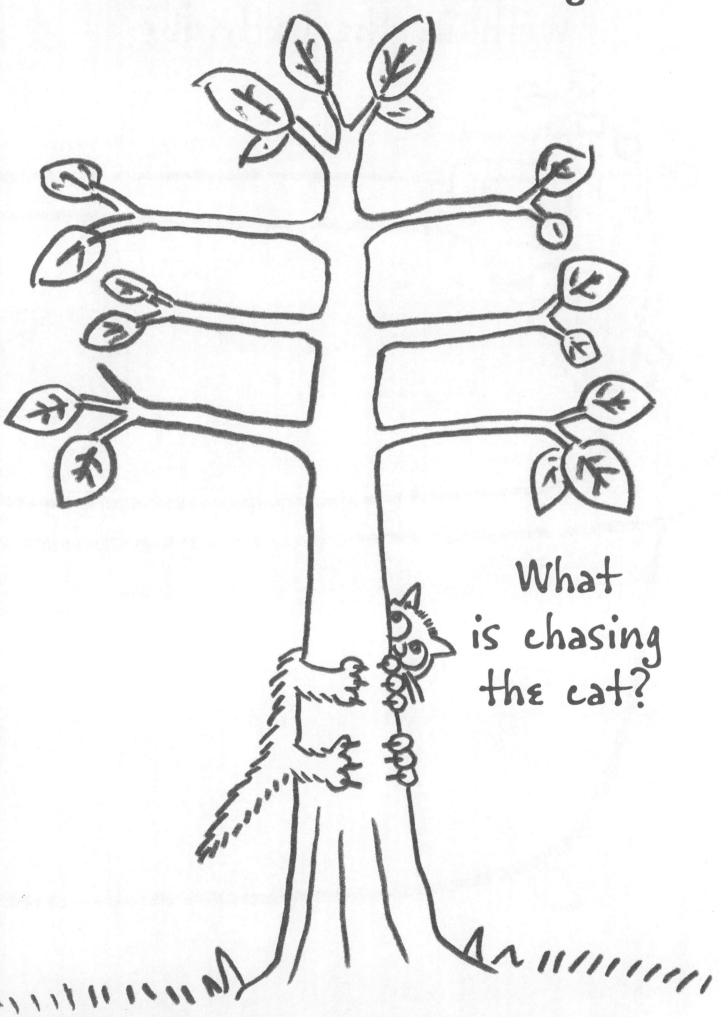

What is chasing the cat?

What do you play with in the bathtub?

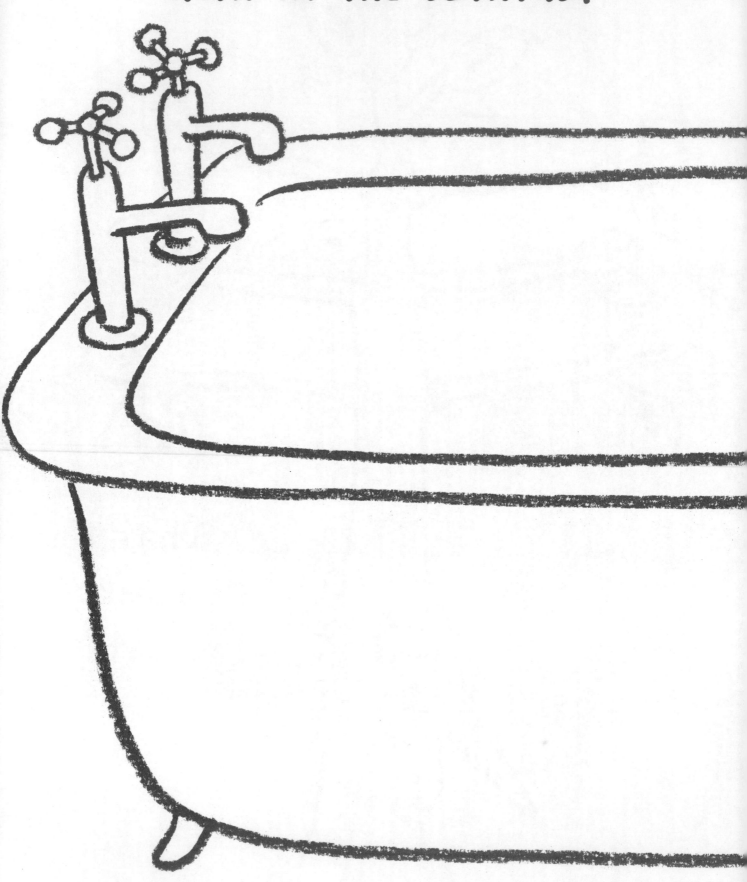

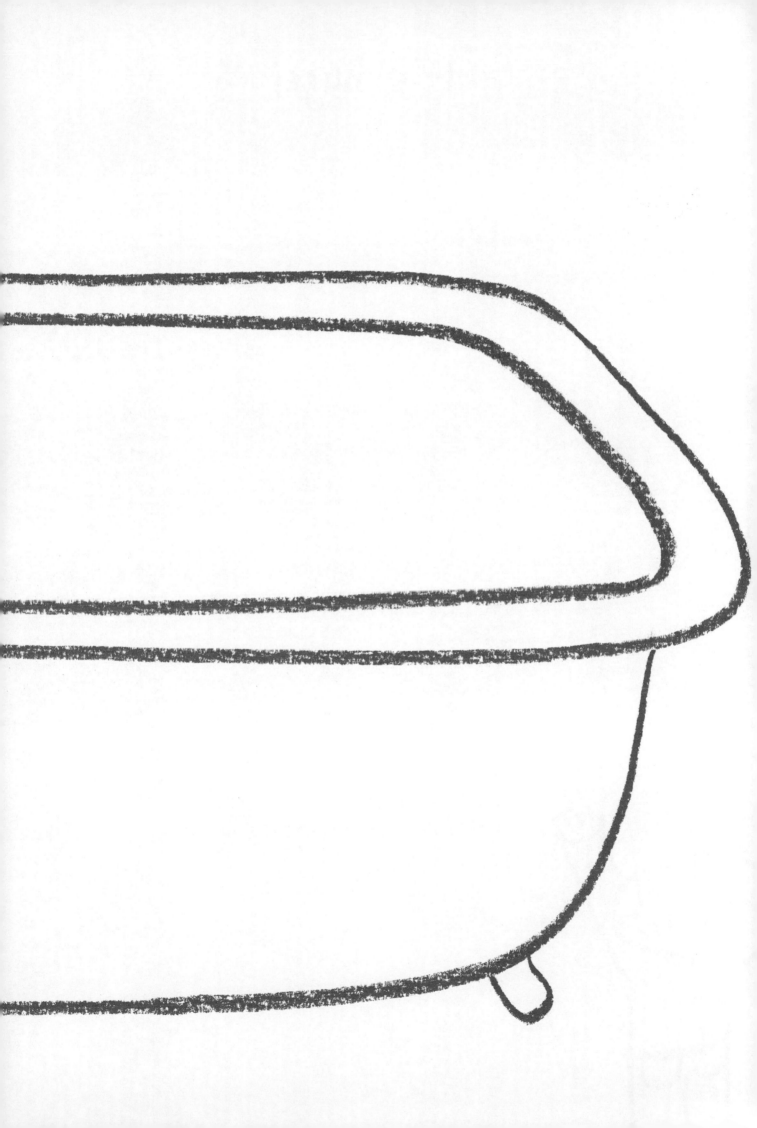

It's huge!

It's huge!

It's tiny!

Whose teeth?

Open the box and
let it loose!

Attach some balloons.

Build a tree house.

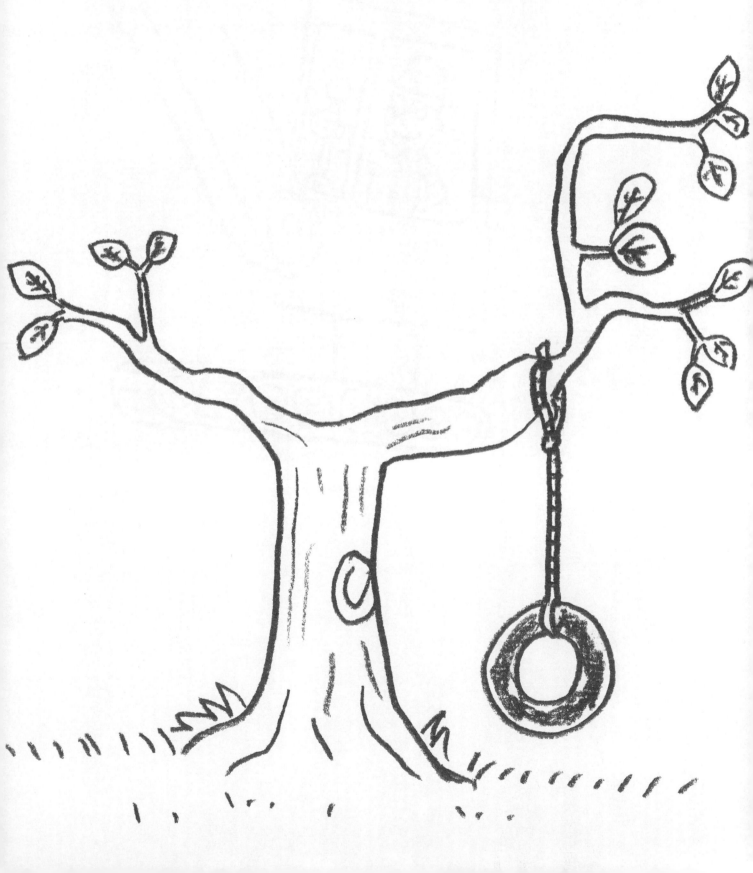

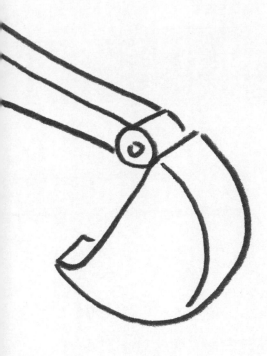

Dig a great big hole.

Finish the pattern.

Set the table.

Fill the bookshelves.

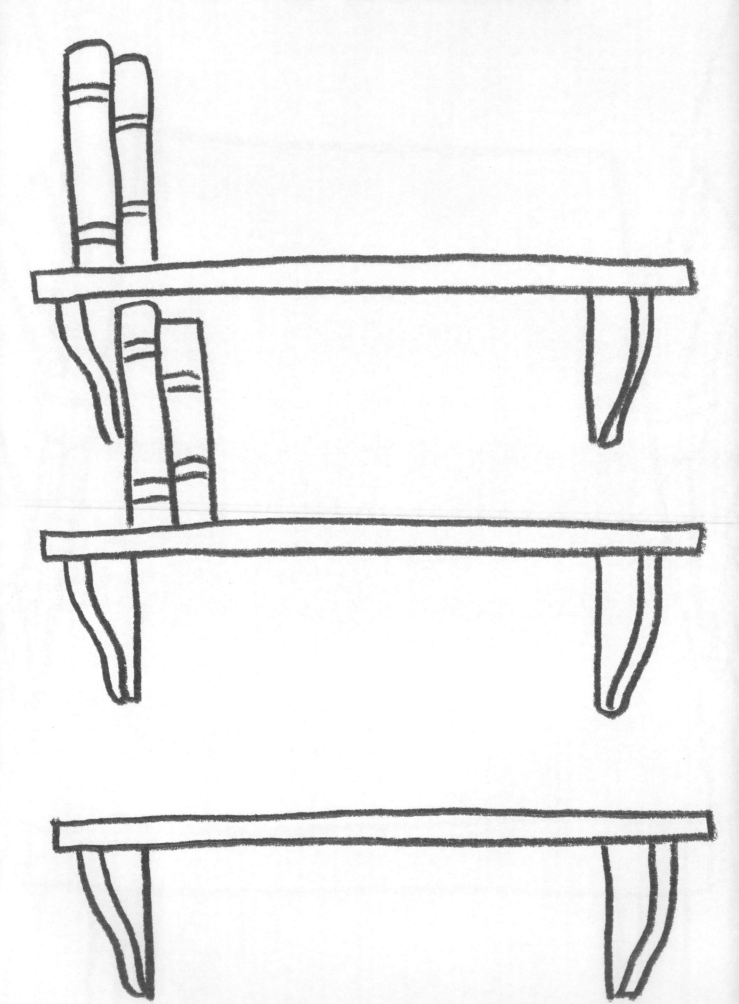

Pin some medals on the General.

Who needs glasses?

Look what you did!

What's under the rock?

Give the penguin some fish.

Fill the chest
with treasure.

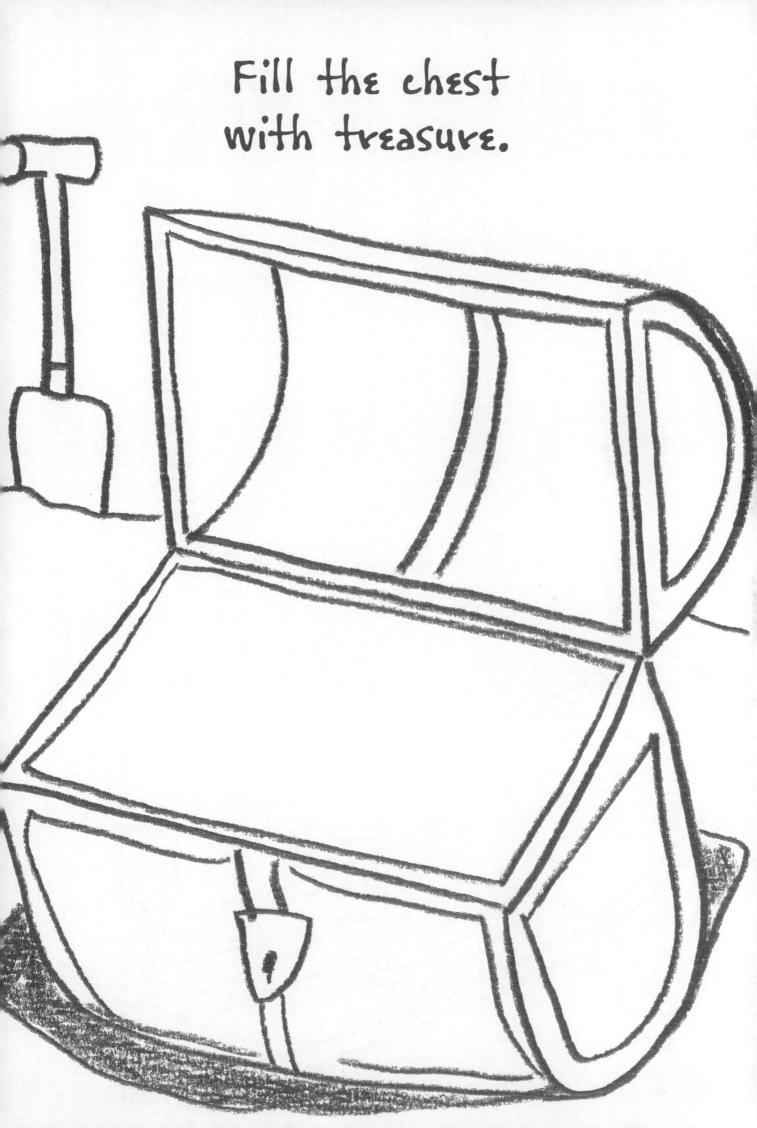

Make the sun shine.

Magic something
from the hat.

Shoot to score!

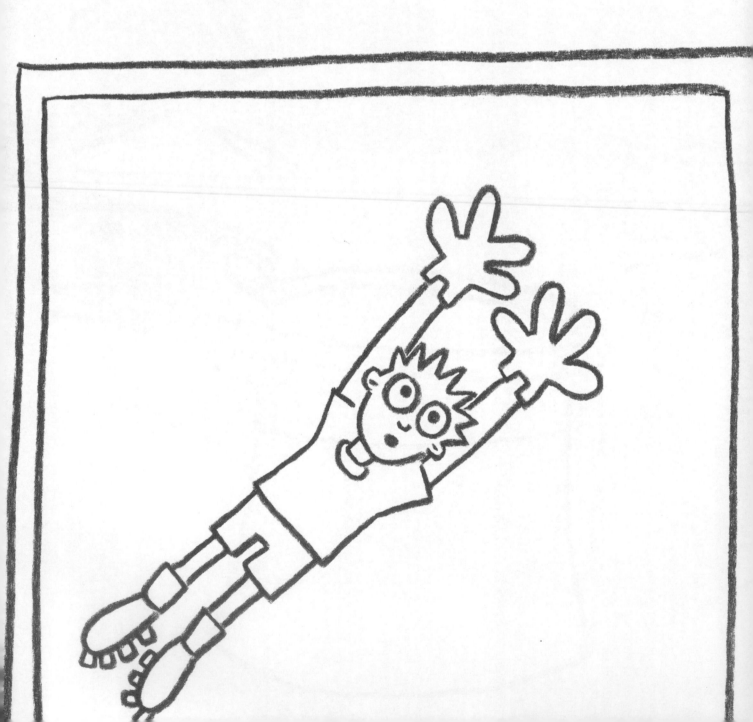

Show the reflection
in the lake.

Make a masterpiece.

What am I pushing?

There was an old lady
who swallowed a....

What's lighter than a feather?

What's on the other side?

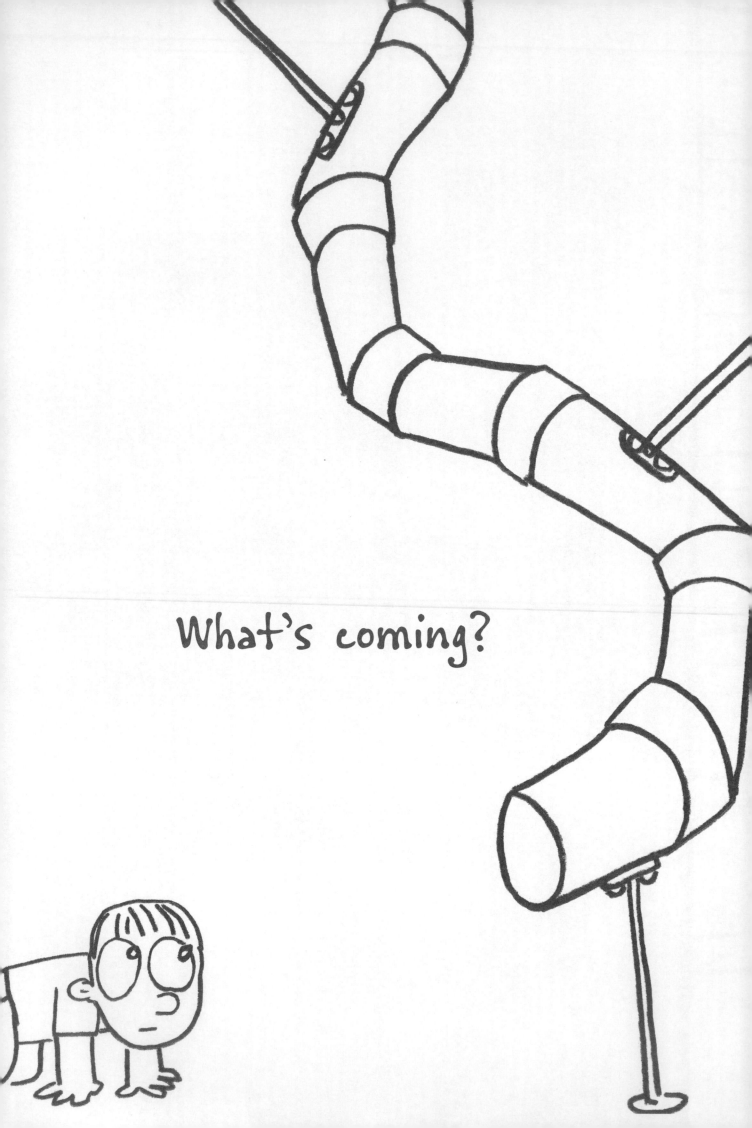

What's coming?

What's heavier than an elephant?

Hang out your wash.

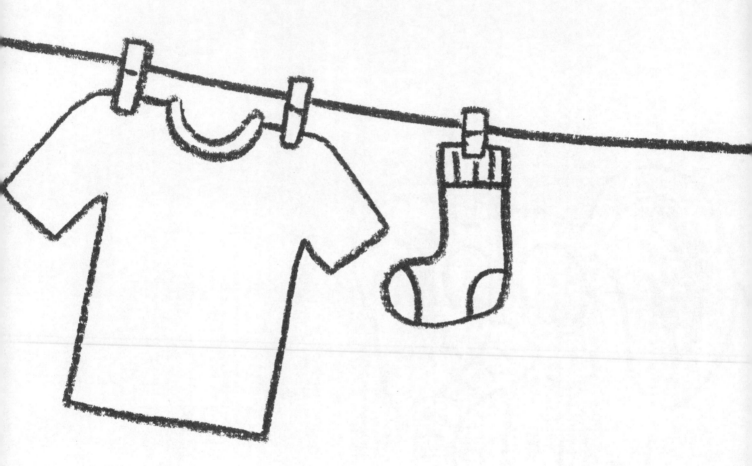

What's for breakfast?

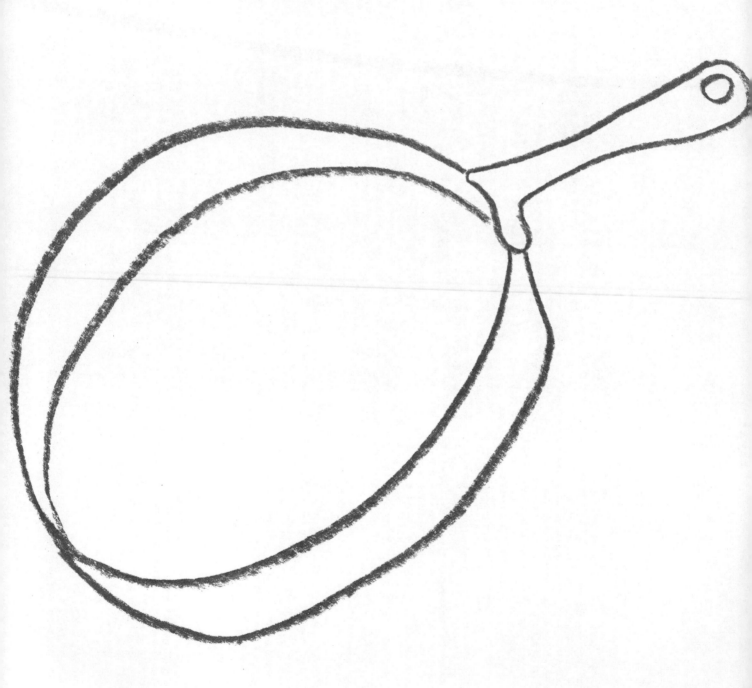

LOST

Make a thunderstorm.

What's growing?

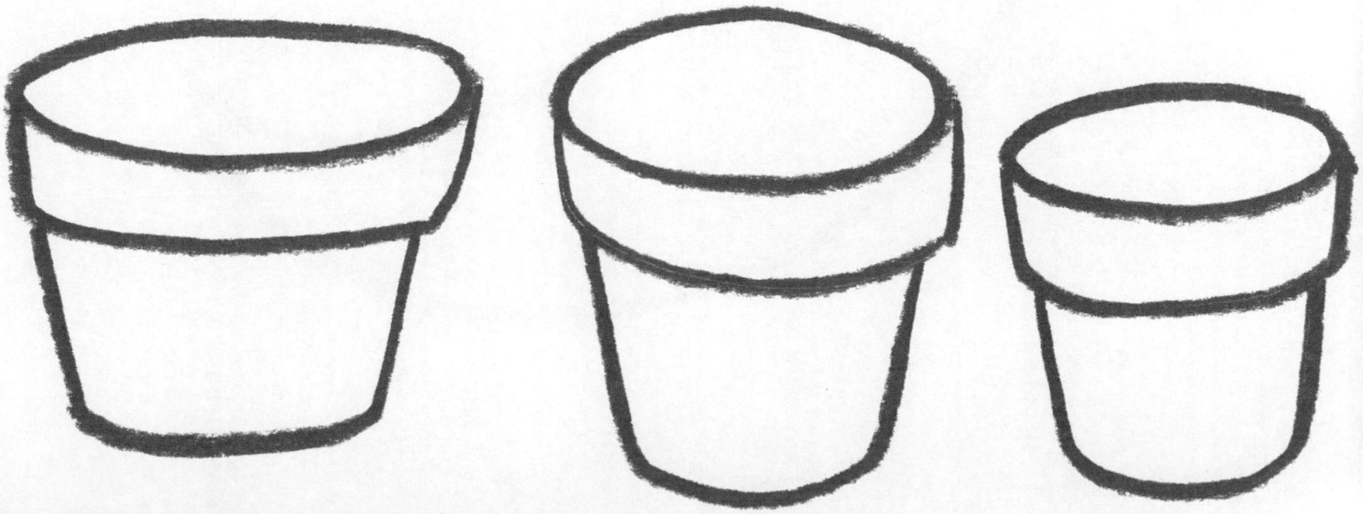

The cow jumped
over the moon.

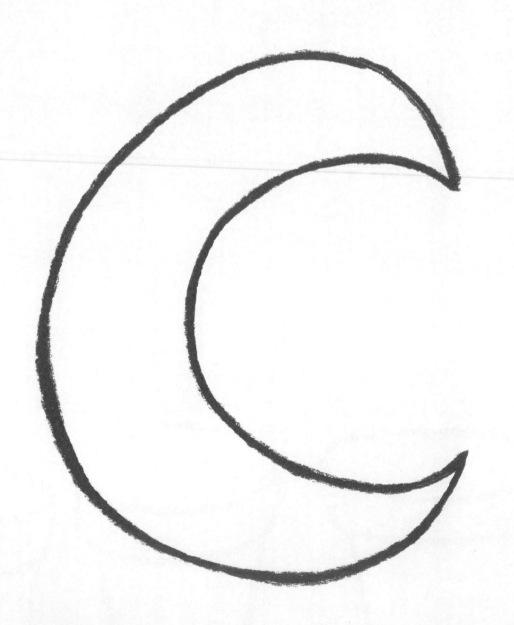

Show my reflection
in the mirror.

What's behind me?

Who are you talking to?

Who walked where?

How many can you juggle?

What did you buy?

Give me some friends.

Tickle me.

What do monsters dream of?

Fill the piggy bank with money.

Magic beanstalks.

Give the birds a tree.

Finish the pattern.

I spy with my little eye
something beginning with D.

What do you wish for?

March them up to
the top of the hill.

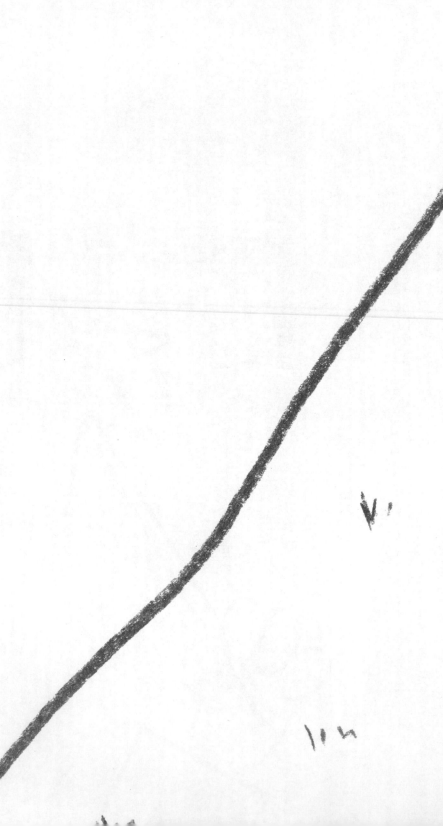

March them
down again.

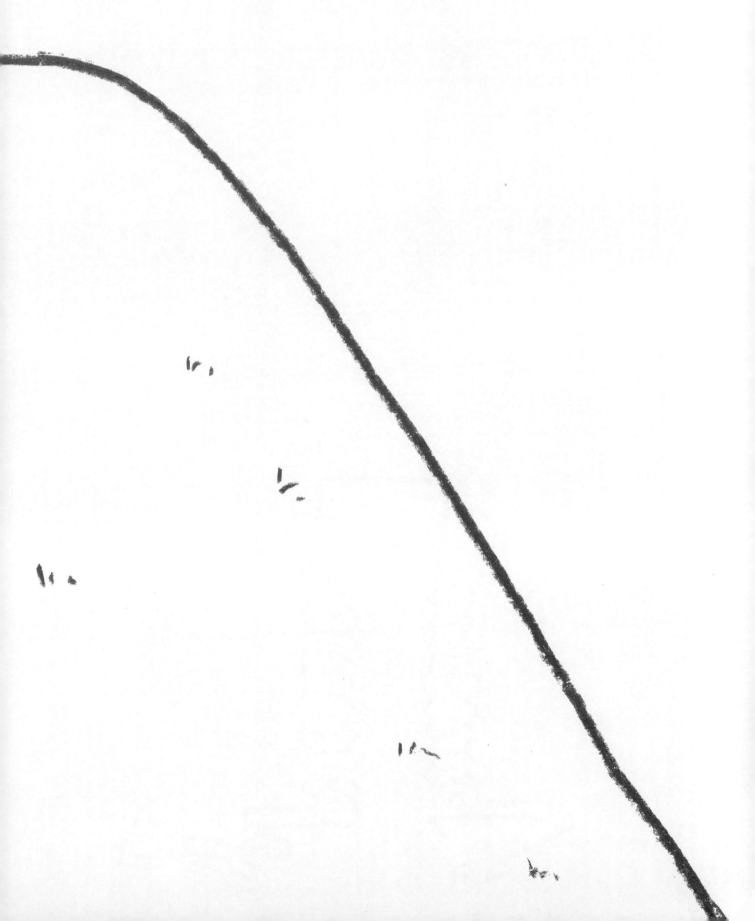

Build a robot.

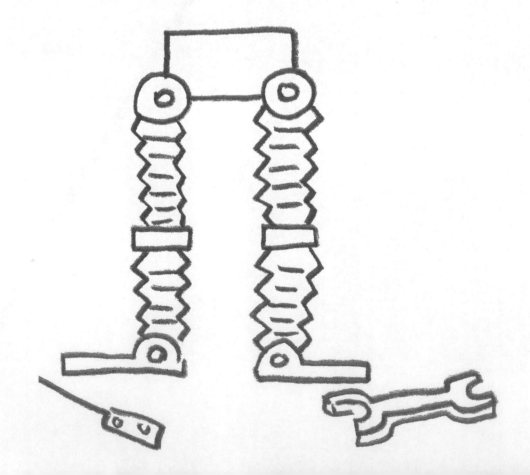

What's on the other end?

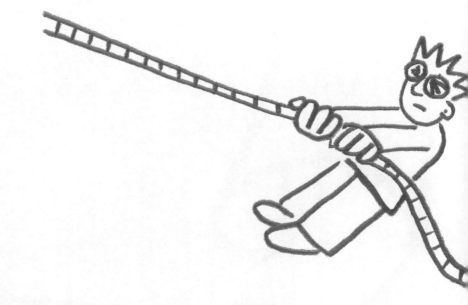

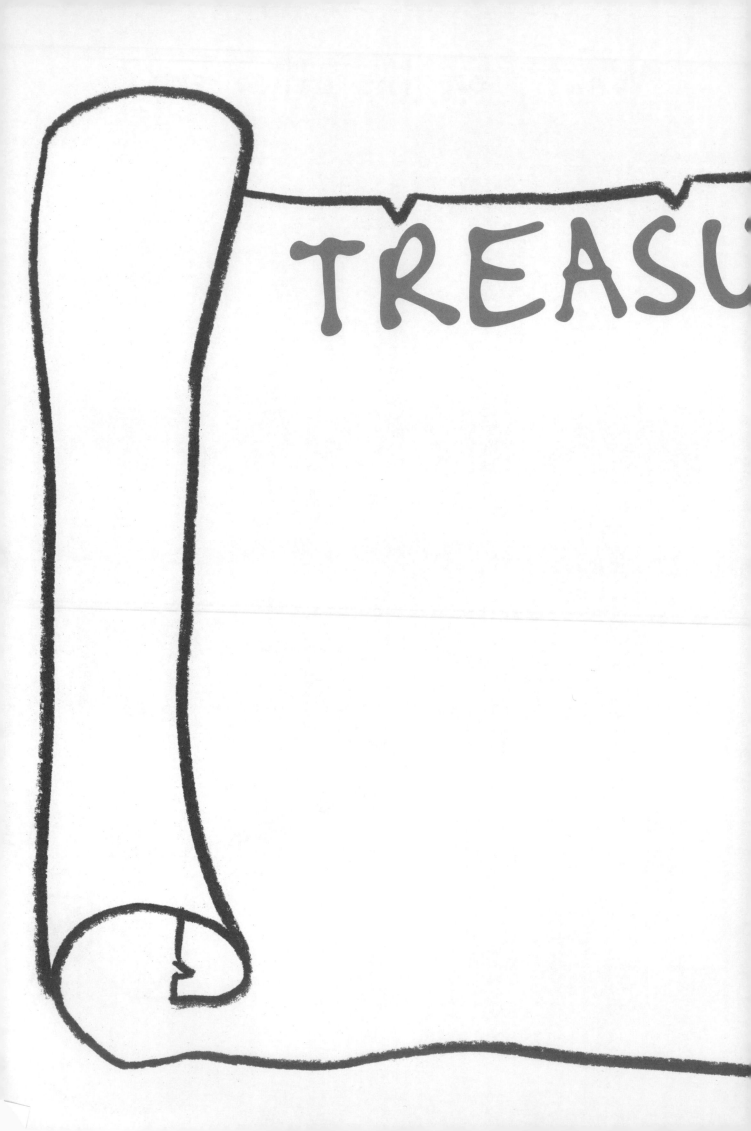

Watch out for the octopus!

Aliens have landed!

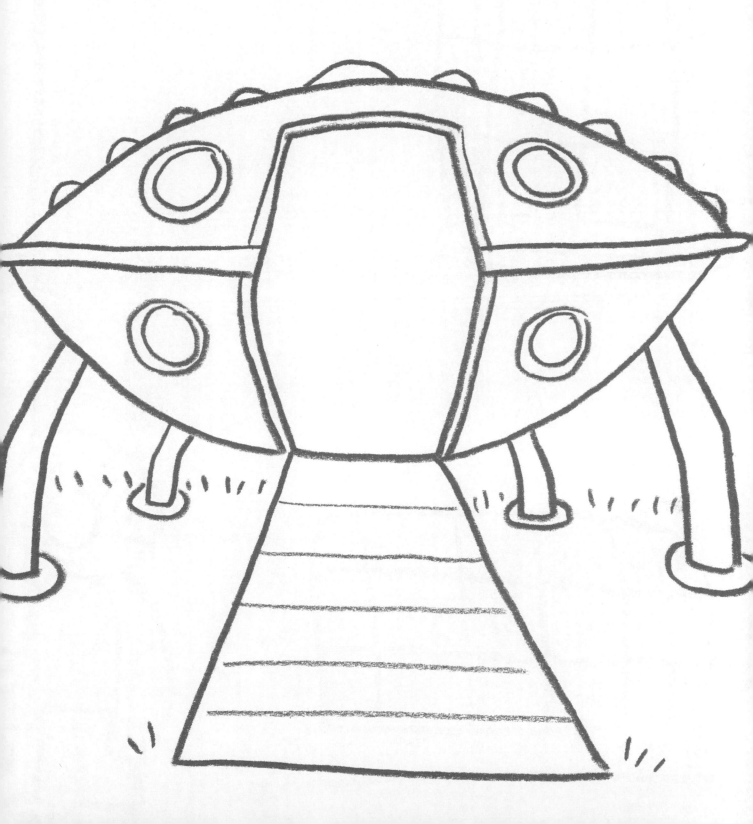

What's in the cages?

It's biting my foot!

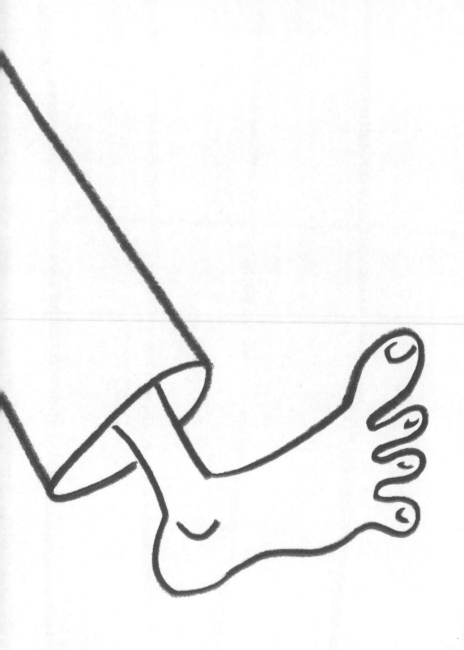

Who's at the windows?

Let them all loose!

What's for sale?

Who's at the door?

What's taller than a giraffe?

Put some stars
in the sky.

Any sharks in the water?

Feed the animals.

What pizza topping would you like?

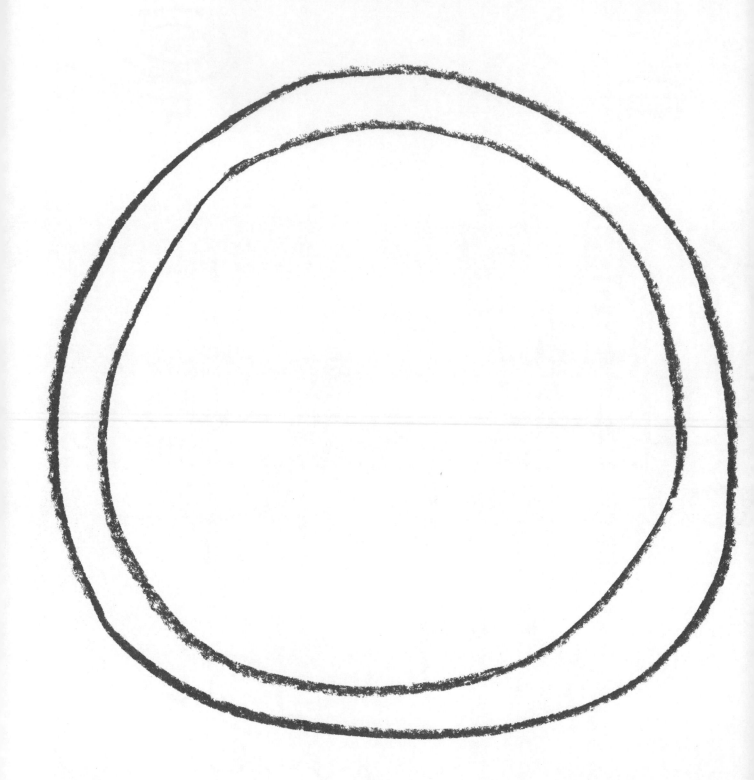

Design and lace the shoe.

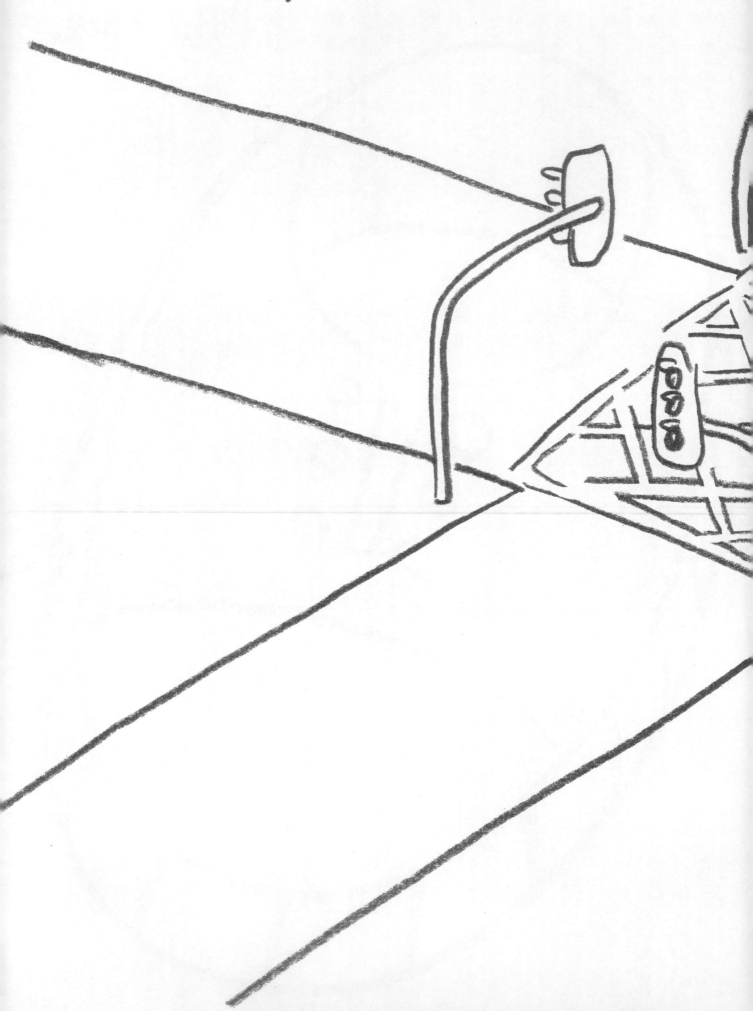

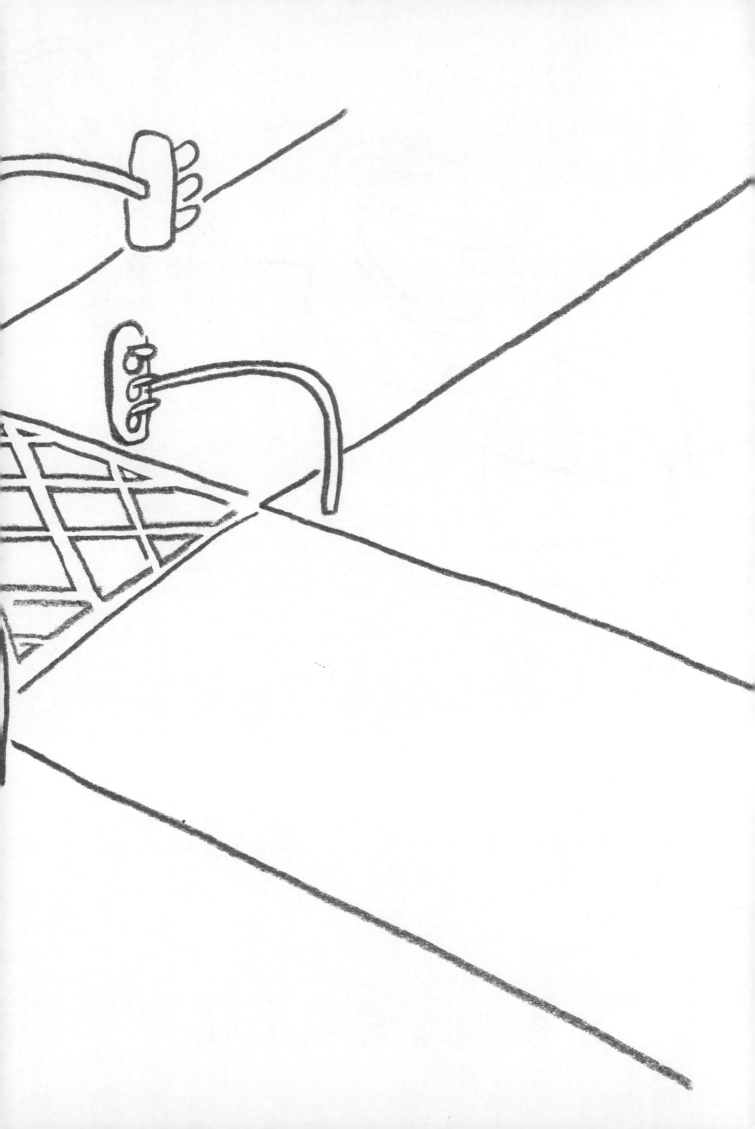

Build a sandcastle.

Finish the pattern.

Who's in the park?

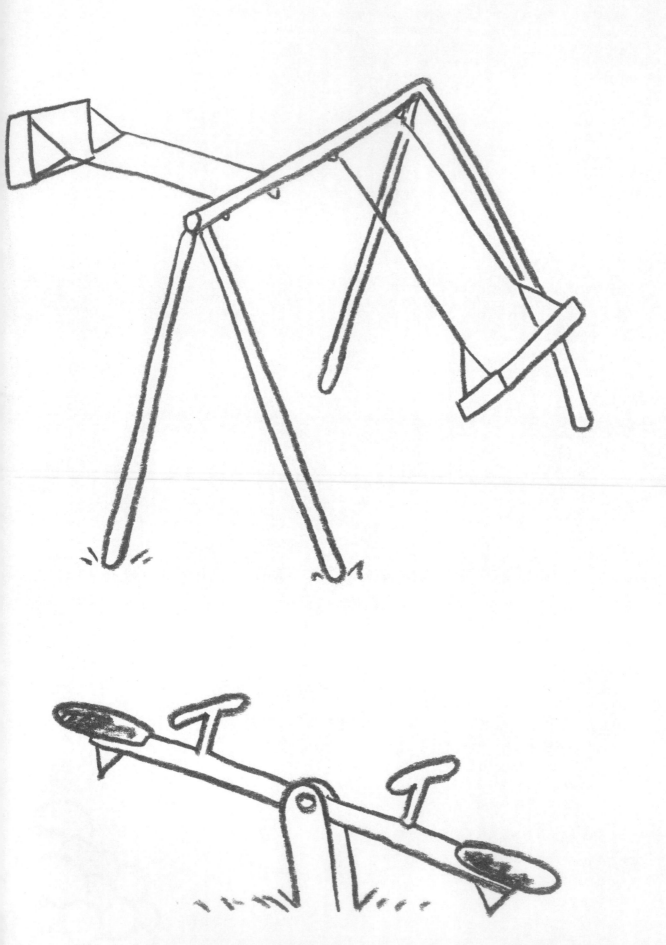

What would you invent?

Give the lady some jewels.

Whose feet?

Make a trap to catch the bad guy.

Knit the world's
longest scarf.

Complete the maze.

Who lives here?

Finish building the city.

What did the window cleaner see?

Dress the snowman
and woman.

Ready for takeoff?

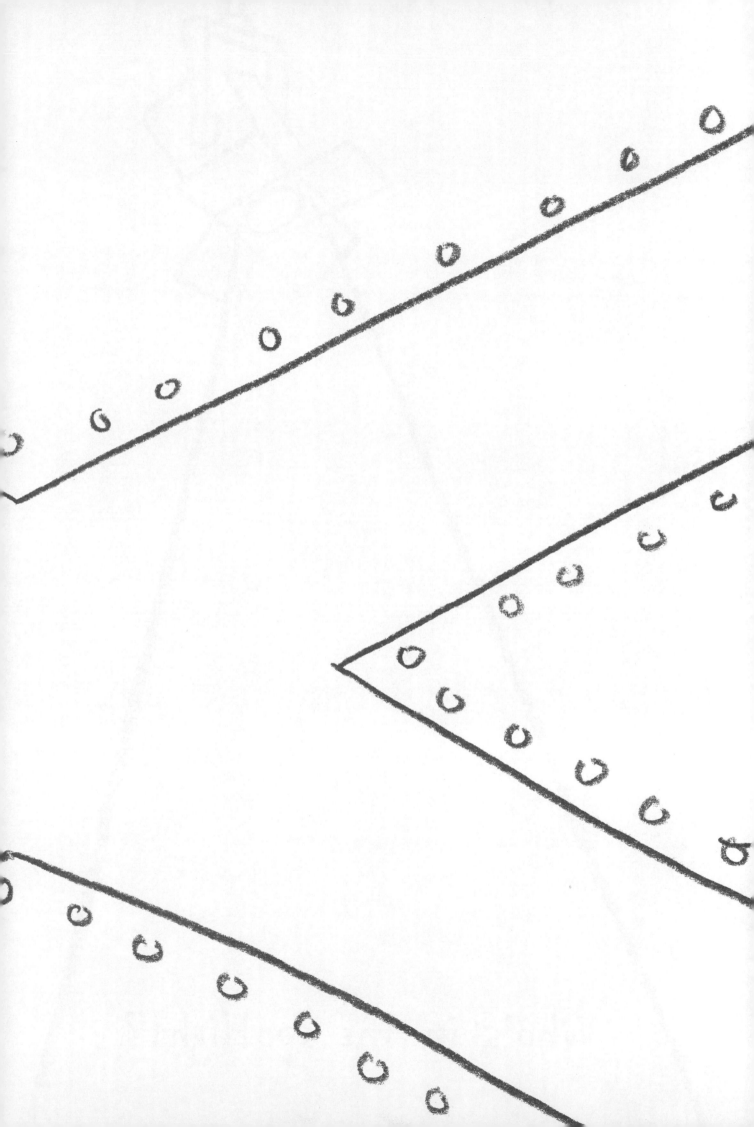

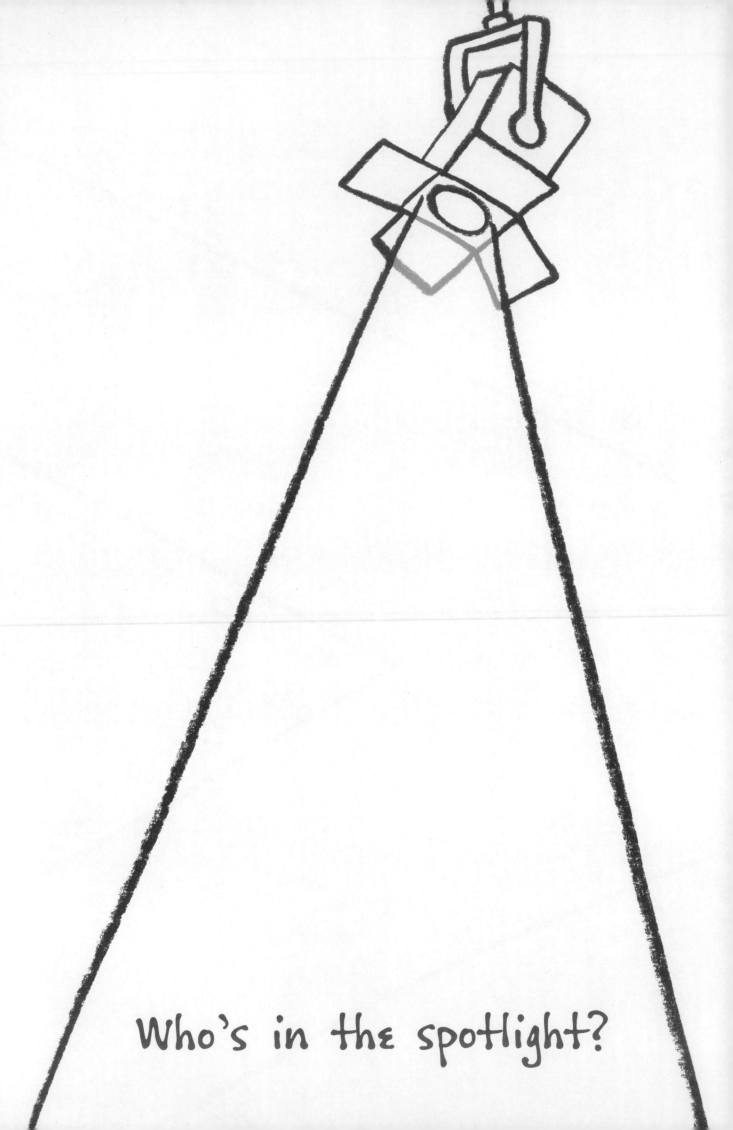

Who's in the spotlight?

Who's in the crowd?

What's in the basement?

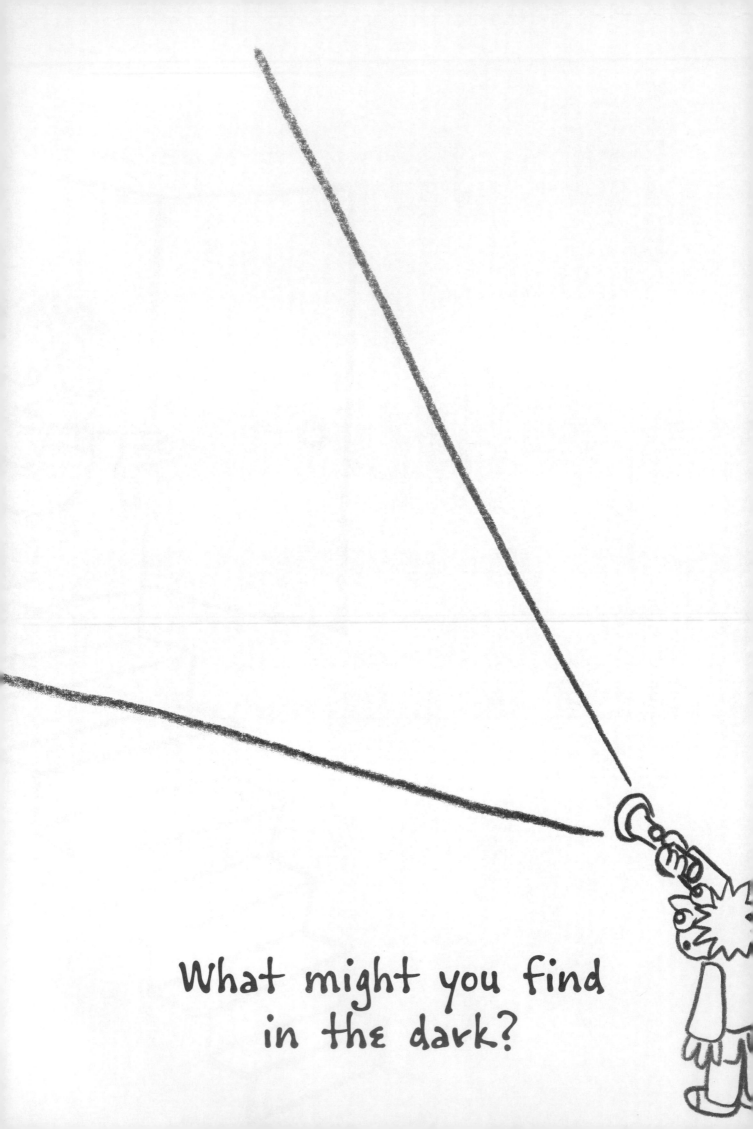

What might you find
in the dark?

Where am I?

Win the race.

Fill the bus.

What's underground?

We're going to a costume party.

Whose hats?

Decorate the tree.

That's a lovely present!

Make a traffic jam.

Who's in
the jungle?

Finish the pattern.

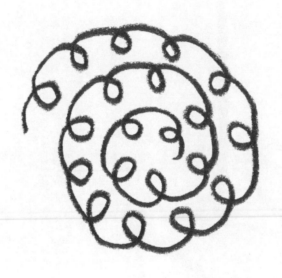

Who's the champion?

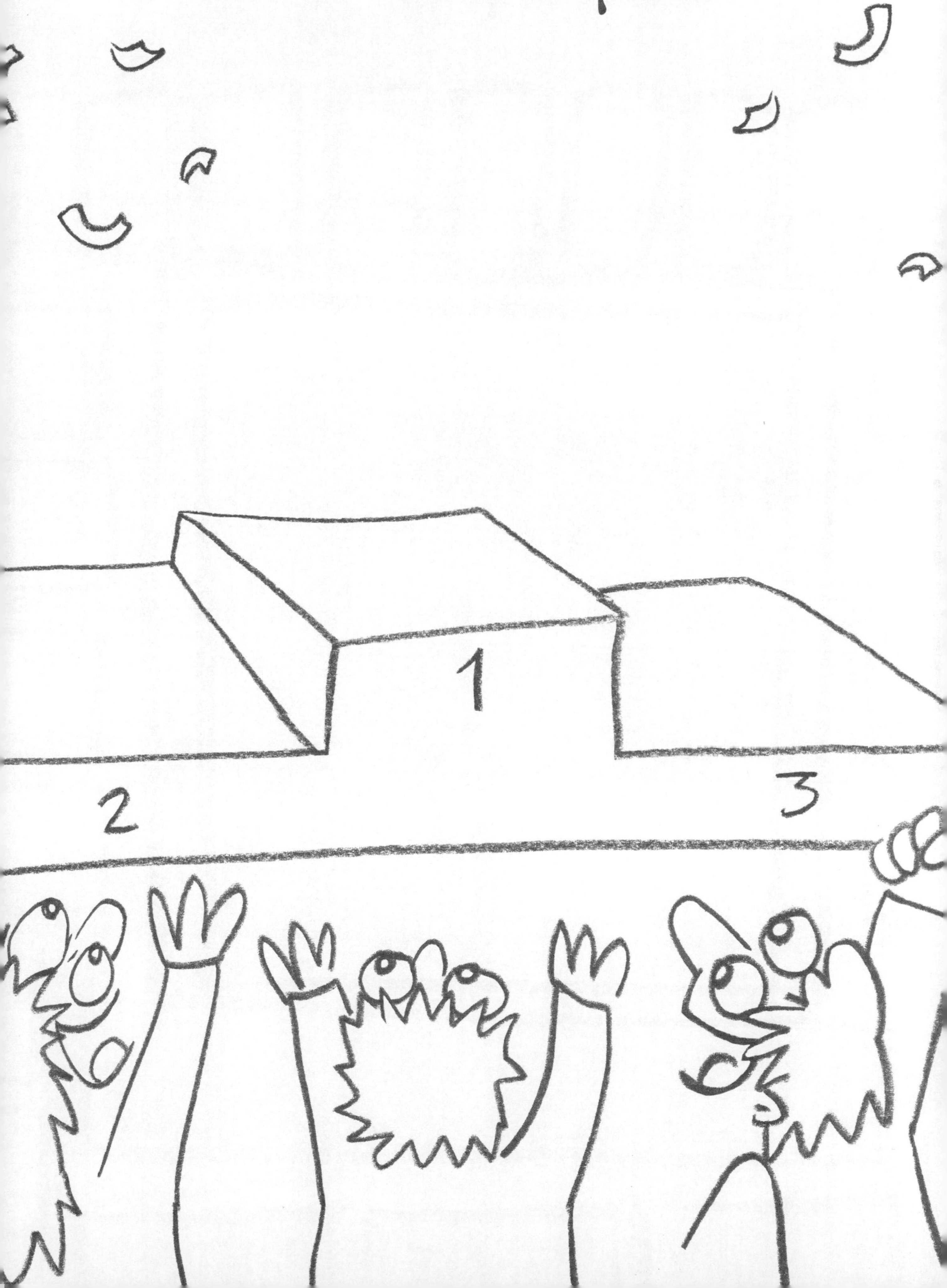

What can you see inside?

What can you see outside?

Where are we going?

What has hatched?

Do some tricks.

Who's playing?

What's coming out of the tunnel?

Why did the chicken cross the road?

Walk the tightrope.

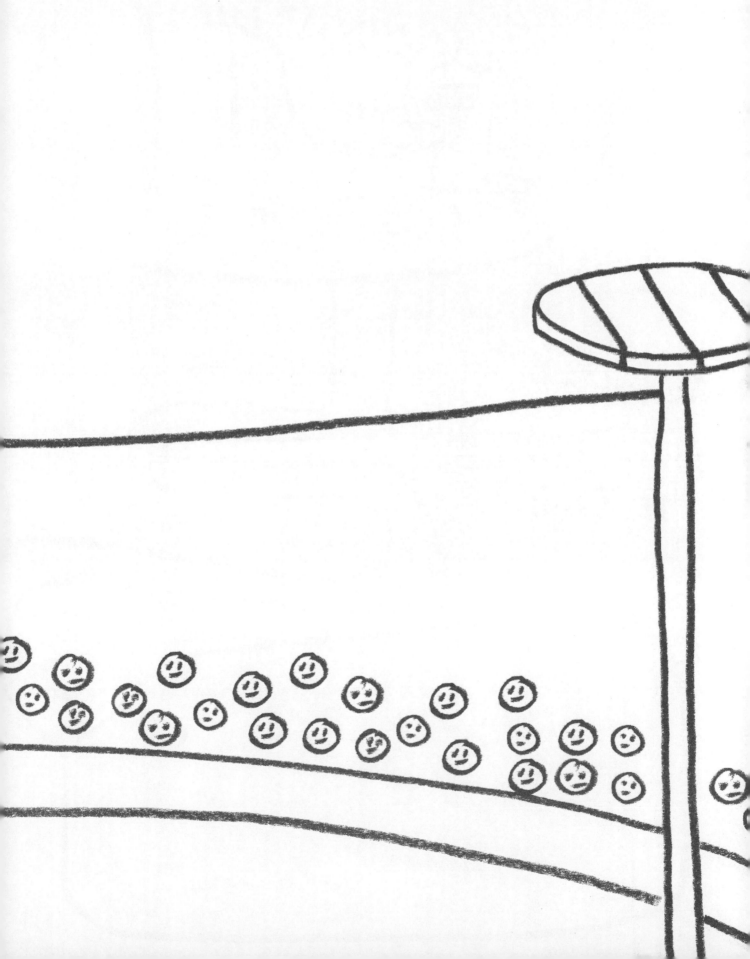

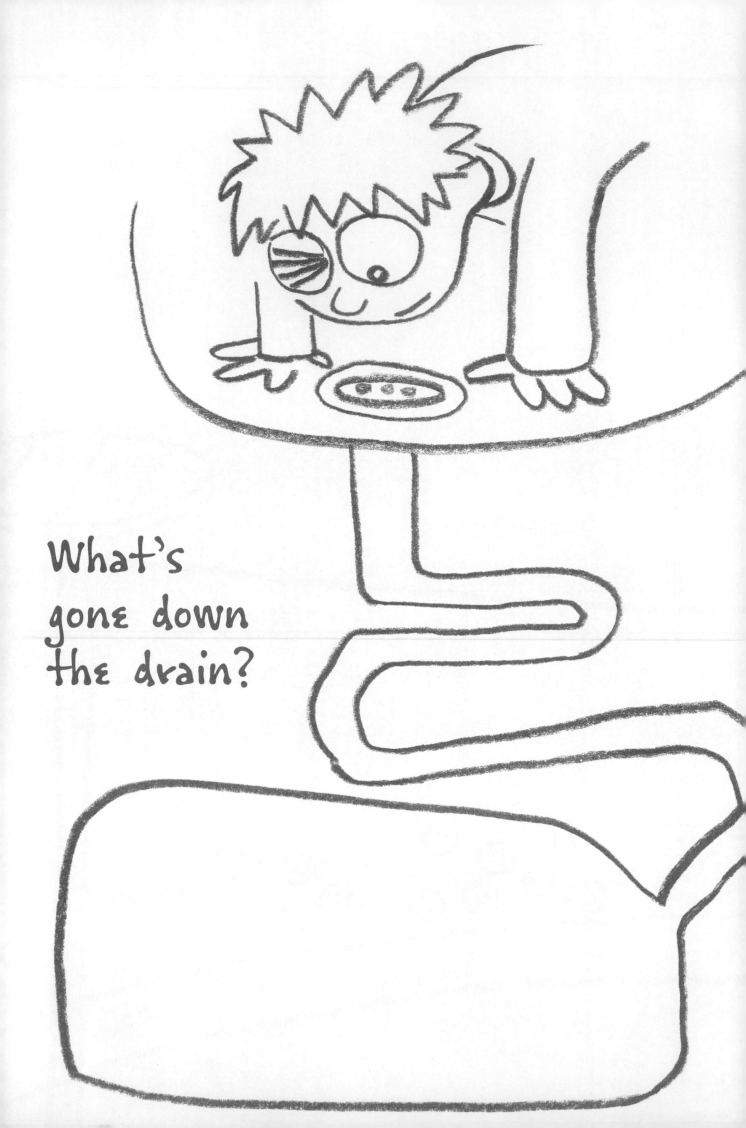

What's gone down the drain?

Here's a baby dinosaur.
But where's its daddy?

WANTED